Official Guide to the

Wales Coast Path: Isle of Anglesey

A complete anti-clockwise circuit of the island from Bangor

Walking along Traeth Penrhos towards Ynys Llanddwyn, Newborough

@WalesCoastPath | @WalesCoastUK
www.walescoastpath.gov.uk | www.walescoastpath.co.uk

Official Guide to the
Wales Coast Path
Isle of Anglesey

A complete anti-clockwise circuit of the island from Bangor

125 miles/ 200 kilometres of superb coastal walking

Carl Rogers

Mara Books
www.northerneyebooks.co.uk

Mara Books

First published in 2025 by:
Mara Books – an imprint of
Northern Eye Books Ltd
22, Crosland Terrace, Helsby, Frodsham Cheshire

Text: Carl Rogers | **Series editor:** Tony Bowerman
Introductory & additional text: Tony Bowerman

Design & photography: Carl Rogers

Additional photographs: Visit Wales, Amgueddfa Cymru / National Museum Wales, Llyfrgell Genedlaethol Cymru / National Library of Wales, Adobe Stock, Shutterstock, Dreamstime, Tony Bowerman

© Mara Books 2025

Carl Rogers has asserted his rights under the Copyright, Designs and Patents Act, 1988 to be identified as the author of this work. All rights reserved.

This book contains mapping data licensed from the Ordnance Survey with the permission of the Controller of Her Majesty's Stationery Office. All maps based on the 1:50,000 Landranger map.

© Crown copyright 2025. All rights reserved. Licence number AC0000833184

email: carl@marabooks.co.uk

For trade and sales enquiries, please call:
01928 723 744

ISBN 978-1-902512-40-2

A CIP catalogue record for this book is available from the British Library

Printed and bound in the UK on wood-friendly FSC stock

Important Advice: The route described in this book is undertaken at the reader's own risk. Walkers should take into account their level of fitness, wear suitable footwear and clothing, and carry food and water. It is also advisable to take the relevant OS maps with you in case you get lost and leave the area covered by our maps.

Whilst every care has been taken to ensure the accuracy of the route directions, the publishers cannot accept responsibility for errors or omissions, or for changes in the details given. Nor can the publisher and copyright owners accept responsibility for any consequences arising from the use of this book.

If you find any inaccuracies in either the text or maps, please write or email us at the addresses below. Thank you.

Acknowledgements: Warm thanks are due to everyone who helped make this book a reality. Thank you, in particular, to Natural Resources Wales' officer Quentin Grimley for his friendly advice and support. Thanks, too, to the many tourism officers, museum and library staff, Wales on View picture researchers, freelance photographers, and everyone else who has played their part. And, finally, thanks to Thomas Leber, end-to-end walker, for his heart-felt quote explaining why the Wales Coast Path is so special.

www.northerneyebooks.co.uk
www.walescoastpath.co.uk

Cyfoeth Naturiol Cymru
Natural Resources Wales

@WalesCoasUK
@CarlMaraBooks

@wales_coast_path
@carlrogers1960

Contents

Wales Coast Path: Discover the shape of a nation 6

Wales Coast Path: An 870-mile coastal adventure 8
The Best of Anglesey 28
Isle of Anglesey: Part of the Wales Coast Path 30
Walking the Anglesey coast — map and distance chart 32
Day Sections 35
Limited for time? Anglesey in a nutshell 42
A brief history of the Isle of Anglesey 44
Wildlife on the Isle of Anglesey 50
Red squirrels, orchids and choughs 52

The Isle of Anglesey section of the Wales Coast Path

Day Section 1: Bangor to Beaumaris 60
Day Section 2: Beaumaris to Pentraeth 68
Day Section 3: Pentraeth to Moelfre 80
Day Section 4: Moelfre to Amlwch Port 88
The 'Golden Wreck' 92
Day Section 5: Amlwch to Cemaes 100
Day Section 6: Cemaes Bay to Church Bay 108
Rocks, Reefs and Shipwrecks 116
Day Section 7: Church Bay to Holyhead 122
Day Section 8: Holyhead to Trearddur 132
Day Section 9: Trearddur to Four-Mile Bridge 142
Day Section 10: Four-Mile Bridge to Aberffraw 150
Sacrificial Lake? 158
Day Section 11: Aberffraw to Newborough 164
Lovers' Island 172
Day Section 12: Newborough to Menai Bridge 176
Menai Strait 182

Wales Coast Path: Official Guides 189
Useful Information 194

Official Guides to the Wales Coast Path

The Official Guides to the Wales Coast Path are endorsed by **Natural Resources Wales,** the body responsible for coordinating the development of the route. The guides split the Path into seven main sections with a guide for each. Together, they cover the entire 870-mile Path from the outskirts of Chester in the north to Chepstow in the south.

For details of the full range of Official Guides to the Wales Coast Path, see:
www.walescoastpath.gov.uk/plan-your-trip/guidebooks

Wales Coast Path
Discover the shape of a nation

Wales is the largest country in the world with a continuous path around its entire coast. The **Wales Coast Path** promises 870 miles/1400 kilometres of unbroken coastal walking, from the outskirts of Chester in the north to Chepstow in the south. Along the way you'll experience the very best of Wales: stunning scenery, stirring history, Welsh culture, and wildlife in abundance. If you tackle only one big walk in your life, make it this one. It's unmissable.

Great Orme, Llandudno

Llancwyfan, Anglesey

Sandwich tern

Harlech Castle, Gwynedd

Aberdyfi, Ceredigion

'Green Bridge of Wales', Pembrokeshire

Rhossili Bay, Gower

Red squirrel

Millennium Centre, Cardiff

Chepstow Castle, Gwent

Wales Coast Path
An 870-mile coastal adventure

When the **Wales Coast Path** opened in May 2012, Wales became the largest country in the world with a continuous path around its entire coast. Walkers can now enjoy unparalleled coastal walking around the Welsh seaboard from top to bottom: from the outskirts of the ancient walled city of Chester, on the Dee estuary in the north, to the pretty market town of Chepstow, on the Severn Estuary, in the south.

The official, signposted and waymarked path covers roughly 870 miles/1400 kilometres and starts and finishes close to the ends of the historic 180 mile/285 kilometre Offa's Dyke National Trail. This means keen walkers can make a complete circumnavigation of Wales; a total distance of around 1,050 miles/1,690 kilometres. Ever keen for a new challenge, a few hardy walkers had already completed the full circuit within months of the Wales Coast Path's opening.

But whether you choose to walk the whole Path in one go, in occasional sections, or a few miles at a time, you're in for a real treat. There's something new around every corner, and you'll discover places that can only be reached on foot. Visually stunning and rich in both history and wildlife, the path promises ever-changing views, soaring cliffs and spacious beaches, sea caves and arches, wildflowers, seabirds, seals and dolphins, as well as castles, cromlechs, coves and coastal pubs. It's a genuinely special landscape.

Ynys Llanddwyn and the hills of Llŷn

This visual and ecological richness is recognised nationally and internationally. In fact, the Wales Coast Path runs through 1 Marine Nature Reserve, 1 Geopark, 2 National Parks, 3 Areas of Outstanding Natural Beauty, 3 World Heritage Sites, 7 official and unofficial nudist beaches, 11 National Nature Reserves, 14 Heritage Coasts, 17 Special Protection Areas, 21 Special Areas of Conservation, 23 Historic Landscapes, 42 Blue Flag beaches, and 111 marine Sites of Special Scientific Interest. Large stretches of coast are also managed and protected by Wildlife Trusts, the RSPB and the National Trust.

Long-distance walkers will enjoy the unbroken path, the solitude, the coast's constantly changing moods and the back-to-nature challenge. Holiday and weekend walkers can recharge their batteries, see something new, and regain a necessary sense of perspective. Families can potter, play and explore. And locals can walk the dog, jog, get fit and rediscover their home patch. Whatever your preferences, the Wales Coast Path promises something for everyone.

> "The most important thing if you go on a trip like this is to forget the hectic pace of everyday life, to get a free mind ... and I would always do it again!."
>
> Thomas Leber, end-to-end Autumn 2013

All or Part?

So, what's the best way to walk the Wales Coast Path? The 870 mile/1400 kilometre route covers the whole of the Welsh seaboard and is the longest and probably the best of all Britain's long-distance challenges.

But of course, not everyone has the time, energy or inclination to walk it all at once. Instead, most people start with a short stretch, discover they love it, and come back for more.

Section by section

1. North Wales Coast
2. Isle of Anglesey
3. Llŷn Peninsula
4. Cardigan Bay/Ceredigion
5. Pembrokeshire Coast Path
6. Carmarthen Bay & Gower
7. South Wales Coast

Wales Coast Path 11

1. North Wales Coast
Chester to Bangor
80 miles/125 kilometres
7 Day Sections

Undulating coast. Vast Dee estuary, traditional seaside towns, limestone headland, and Conwy mountain

2. Isle of Anglesey
Circuit of island from Menai Bridge
125 miles/200 kilometres
12 Day Sections

Grand coastal scenery from tidal straits to bays, estuaries, dunes and cliffs. Area of Outstanding Natural Beauty

3. Llŷn Peninsula
Bangor to Porthmadog
110 miles/180 kilometres
9 Day Sections

Unspoilt peninsula with bays, coves and cliffs, tipped by Bardsey Island. Area of Outstanding Natural Beauty

4. Cardigan Bay/Ceredigion
Porthmadog to Cardigan
140 miles/225 kilometres
12 Day Sections

Low-lying dunes and big estuaries followed by steeper, grassy sea cliffs with dramatic coves and bays

5. Pembrokeshire
Cardigan to Tenby/Amroth
185 miles/300 kilometres
14 Day Sections

Varied, beautiful, popular. The Pembrokeshire Coastal Path is a National Trail and coastal National Park

6. Carmarthen Bay & Gower
Tenby to Swansea
131 miles/210 kilometres
12 Day Sections

Long sandy beaches, tidal estuaries, dramatic rocky coast. Area of Outstanding Natural Beauty

7. South Wales Coast
Swansea to Chepstow
115 miles/185 kilometres
11 Day Sections

Traditional beach resorts, seafaring and industrial landscapes. Heritage Coast, National Nature Reserves

Limestone splendour: *Looking towards the Great Orme, on the North Wales coast*

Wales: Top to bottom

Walking the whole 870 miles/1400 kilometres of the Wales Coast Path in one go is an increasingly popular challenge. Some people have even run all the way. By a curious coincidence, the overall distance is almost exactly the same as Britain's famous top-to-bottom route, from John o' Groats to Land's End—a very long way.

The Wales Coast Path will take you from the outskirts of Chester down the broad Dee estuary, along the North Wales coast with its traditional seaside resorts and impressive limestone headlands at the Little Orme and Great Orme, past Conwy Castle, over Conwy Mountain and on along the wooded Menai Strait. The Path then loops around the rugged, offshore Isle of Anglesey, or Ynys Môn, passes the walled town of Caernarfon and its castle before heading around the remote Llŷn Peninsula with Bardsey Island balanced at its tip. From Criccieth and Porthmadog the Path pushes south past Harlech castle—kissing the western rim of the Snowdonia National Park—and on down the majestic sweep of Cardigan Bay with its beautiful, open estuaries. It then rounds Pembrokeshire—Britain's only coastal National Park—with its

sparkling bays and lofty cliffs. Striding through Carmarthenshire and crossing the wide Towy and Tâf estuaries, the Path curves around the lovely Gower Peninsula into Swansea Bay. Beyond the striking Glamorgan Heritage Coast, the Path runs along the Cardiff Bay waterfront to Cardiff, the lively capital of Wales. From there, it's only a short stretch alongside the broad Severn estuary to the pretty market town of Chepstow on the Welsh-English border and the southern end of the Wales Coast Path.

Only the fittest, most determined walkers can hope to complete the entire Path in 6-7 weeks, averaging 20 or so miles a day.

At a more leisurely pace—allowing time to soak up the atmosphere and enjoy the views, and with regular pauses to watch the wildlife, swim, enjoy a quiet drink or visit some of the fascinating places along the way—you should allow around 3 months for the whole trip.

Remember, though, the Wales Coast Path is a challenging route with plenty of rough ground, narrow paths and ups-and-downs (an overall total ascent and descent of 95,800 feet/ 29,200 metres). There are tempting detours and places to see along the way, too. So it's perhaps best to plan slightly shorter and more realistic daily distances than you might ordinarily cover.

You should also allow extra time for the unexpected, to rest or to hole up in bad weather. As a rule of thumb, it's better to be ahead of schedule, with time to enjoy the experience, rather than always having to push ahead to reach the next overnight stop.

The Official Guidebooks in this series break the path down into seven main sections (see the map on page 10), each of which is then sub-divided into carefully-planned 'Day Sections'—usually averaging around 10-15 miles each. These typically start and finish either in, or near easy-to-reach towns, villages or settlements, many of them on bus routes, and with shops, pubs, restaurants, cafés and places to stay nearby.

No matter how long it takes, walking the whole of the Wales Coast Path is a real achievement. For most of us, it would be the walk of a lifetime.

Walking around Wales a bit at a time

Yet, understandably, most people don't want to walk the whole path in one go. Instead, they prefer to do it bit by bit, often over several years: during annual and bank holidays, over long weekends, or as the whim takes them. Done in this leisurely fashion, the walk becomes a project to ponder, plan, and take pleasure in.

A popular way to enjoy the path is to book a short holiday close to a section of the path, and do a series of day walks along the surrounding coast, returning to your base each night.

South Stack lighthouse, on the north-west coast of Anglesey

Sacred Isle?: *Looking across the Sound to Bardsey Island, or Ynys Enlli, at the tip of Llŷn*

Some people like to catch a train (especially along the North Wales Coast), bus or taxi to the start of their day's walk and then walk back (see the information at the start of each day section).

Another approach is to drive to the end of your planned section and then get a pre-booked local taxi to take you back to the start; this costs only a few pounds and lets you walk in one direction at your own pace.

If you're planning to walk a section over several days before returning to your starting point by bus or train, call Traveline on 0870 6082608 or visit **www.traveline-cymru.org.uk** for help with timetables and itineraries.

Best time to go?

Britain's main walking season runs from Easter to the end of September. Although the Wales Coast Path is delightful throughout the year, the best walking weather tends to be in late spring as well as early and late summer.

Although the Easter holiday is busy, spring is otherwise a quiet time of year. The days are lengthening and the weather getting steadily warmer. Migrant birds and basking sharks are returning to Wales from farther south. The weather is also likely to be dry.

Early summer is ideal for walking. May and June enjoy the greatest

Natural beauty: *Rain showers approach the dunes of Morfa Harlech National Nature Reserve*

number of sunshine hours per day (the average for May is 225 hours, and for June 210 hours) and the lowest rainfall of the year (average for May is 50mm, June is 51mm). You'll also have the accompaniment of a spectacular array of spring flowers and the chance to see breeding sea birds at their best.

High summer is the busiest season, particularly during the school holidays in July and August. Both the beaches and the Coast Path are likely to be packed in places. Finding somewhere to stay at short notice can be tricky, too—so it's best to book well in advance. However, the long sunny days are certainly attractive, and you can often walk in shorts and a T-shirt.

By September most visitors have returned home, and you'll have the Coast Path largely to yourself. The weather remains good and the sea is still warm enough for swimming. Sunny days often stretch into September, with the first of the winter storms arriving in late September and October. Autumn also means the coastal trees and bracken are slowly turning from green to red, orange and gold.

Winter brings shorter, colder days with less sunlight and other disadvantages: unpredictable weather, stormy seas, high winds and even gales along with closed cafés and accommodation. But for experienced walkers,

the cooler days can bring peace and solitude and a heightened sense of adventure.

Welsh weather

Like the rest of Britain, Wales is warmed by the Gulf Stream's ocean current and enjoys a temperate climate. This is particularly true of the country's west coast. Because Wales lies in the west of Britain, the weather is generally mild but damp. Low pressure fronts typically come in off the Irish Sea from the west and southwest, hitting the coast first and then moving inland to the east. This means rain and wet weather can occur at any time of year, so you should always take good waterproofs and spare clothes with you.

For more weather or a five-day forecast, visit **www.metoffice.com** or **www.bbc.co.uk/weather**. Several premium-rate national 'Weatherlines' give up-to-date forecasts, and the Snowdonia and Pembrokeshire National Parks websites provide local information, too.

Which direction?

The Official Guide books give directions from north to south, starting in Chester and ending in Chepstow. This means walkers will enjoy the sun on their faces for much of the way. Most luggage transfer services also run in this direction. Nonetheless, the path can be tackled in either direction. It's just easier to go with the flow.

Which section?

Choosing which part of the Wales Coast Path to walk depends in part on where you live, how long you've got, and the kind of scenery you prefer.

Sections vary considerably. Arry Beresford-Webb, the first person to run the entire Path in 2012 said, 'I was stunned by the diversity of the Path. Each section felt like I was going through a different country.'

Some stretches are fairly wild, while others are more developed. Parts of the Isle of Anglesey, Llŷn Peninsula, Cardigan Bay and Pembrokeshire are often remote and away from large settlements. Other stretches, such as North Wales or the South Wales coast around Swansea, Cardiff and Newport are busier, and often close to popular seaside towns or industry.

The terrain varies too. Much of the North Wales coast is low-lying but punctuated with occasional headlands; as are much of Cardigan Bay, Carmarthen Bay, and parts of the Glamorgan Heritage Coast.

In contrast, the Isle of Anglesey, Llŷn Peninsula, Pembrokeshire and Gower are often rocky with high sea cliffs, dramatic headlands, offshore islands and intimate coves.

Self sufficient or supported?

The other key decision for walkers is whether to arrange everything yourself or let experts do it for you. For many people, devising their own itinerary and working out how to travel and where to stay is part of the fun. Others prefer to let one of the specialist walking holiday companies create the itinerary, book accommodation, arrange luggage transfers, meals, and side trips. The main companies are listed at the back of the book.

Accommodation

There are plenty of places to stay within easy reach of the Wales Coast Path all around Wales. Most walkers either camp or stay in bed and breakfast accommodation; usually a mix of the two, thankfully, there are plenty of hostels, campsites and bunkhouses along the way.

Accommodation may be fully booked during peak holiday seasons, so it's advisable to book well in advance. Local Tourist Information Centres (TICs) will often know all the local accommodation providers and can help with booking. For late, or emergency on the spot bookings, it's also worth contacting the TICs listed at the start of each day section.

For online booking visit: www.walescoastpath.co.uk. This website has a specific section for planning your walk, which includes booking a range of accommodation options at the end of each **Day Section**.

Backpacking

Backpacking adds an extra dimension to the walking experience: being outdoors for days at a time, watching the sunrise and sunset, gazing at the stars overhead without artificial light getting in the way. But don't underestimate how much a heavy pack can slow you down. The secret is to travel as light as possible; the lightest tent or bivvi bag, a lightweight sleeping bag and waterproofs, and a single change of clothes.

There are plenty of official campsites along the busier sections of the Wales Coast Path. However, many are on small farms and may not advertise. Elsewhere campsites are often few and far between, and may need searching for. During peak season some may also be full, so it's advisable to book ahead. But remember, most sites are closed during the winter (typically from November to Easter, and often longer).

The sandy mouth of the Dyfi Estuary reaches out towards Aberdyfi

Unofficial 'wild camping' is a grey area. There is no legal right in England or Wales to 'wild camp' anywhere, including alongside the path. Every scrap of land in Britain belongs to someone, and many landowners frown on campers. So it makes sense to ask before pitching.

Unofficially, however, overnight camping is usually tolerated, so long as you pitch a small tent unobtrusively in the evening, and pack up and leave early the next morning, without leaving a trace.

Alternatively, there are popular luggage transfer services on the more established stretches of the Path. For a small fee, they wiil pick up your rucksack and other bags and transport them to the end of your day's walk. A list of luggage transfer companies appears at the back of the book.

One of the many remote coves in the north-west corner of the island

Well equipped: *Two well equipped walkers on the coastal path approach Borth Wen, near Cemlyn*

Clothes, boots and backpack

For those new to long distance walking, it's worth emphasising the benefits of comfortable walking boots and suitable clothing. Walking continuously, day after day, puts extra pressures on your feet. Be prepared for changes in the weather, too. Carry waterproofs and remember that several thin layers allow you to adjust your clothing as conditions change.

Checking the weather forecast before you set off each day will help you decide what to wear. If you're in the car, it's worth taking a selection of clothing for different conditions, and deciding what to wear and carry immediately before you start.

Onshore breezes can mask the strength of the sun. To avoid sunburn, or even sunstroke, remember to slap on some sunscreen and wear a hat.

Other things to take, depending on weight, include: maps, water bottle, lightweight walking poles, basic First Aid including plasters and antiseptic cream, penknife, head torch and spare batteries, chocolate, sweets or energy bars, toilet paper, a small camera, binoculars, mobile phone, and a pen and notebook. Don't forget some spare cash too; most places accept cards but finding a Cashpoint or somewhere that offers 'Cash Back' near the Path can be tricky.

Outdoor dining: *Anglesey has many excellent coastal pubs—The Oystercatcher, Rhosneigr*

Food and drink

Although the official guidebooks try to start and end each day at places with amenities, some sections are nonetheless remote and may have few places to buy food or drink. This may be the case for several days in a row. So it makes sense to plan ahead and carry enough supplies with you. Conversely, other sections are well supplied with shops, pubs, cafés, restaurants and takeaways, and these are indicated at the start of each Day Section.

Maps

The maps in this book are based on the Ordnance Survey Landranger 1:50,000 series, with the line of the Wales Coast Path highlighted in orange. The numbers on the maps correspond to those in the route description for each day section.

Wales Coast Path map booklet

The best maps for walking are the larger scale, Ordnance Survey Explorer 1:25,000 scale maps, which show additional features such as Access Land, and field boundaries. Both scales of OS maps now have the official route of the Wales Coast Path marked on them: as a line composed of a series of red diamonds on the 1:50,000 Landranger maps, and green diamonds on the 1:25,000 Explorer maps.

The relevant maps for each Day Section are listed at the beginning of each chapter. **Northern Eye Books** also publish a **handy map** for each section of the Path in booklet format using the 1:25,000 Ordnance Survey maps. These are smaller and easier to use than large sheet maps. To buy online visit: www.northerneyebooks.co.uk or www.walescoastpath.co.uk.

Route finding

For the most part, the Wales Coast Path follows a single official route. In a few places, there are both official and unofficial alternative routes. Otherwise, the path hugs the coast as far is practically and legally possible, occasionally diverting inland around private estates, nature reserves, natural obstacles, estuaries, gunnery ranges and so on. The definitive route, and any occasional changes are notified on the official Wales Coast Path website.

The path uses a mixture of public rights of way: footpaths, bridleways and byways as well as lanes, open access land, beaches and some permissive paths. On most sections, the route is well-used and clear. In remote or under-used areas, however, walkers will need to pay closer attention to the maps and directions in this book.

Fingerposts and waymarkers

The Wales Coast Path is clearly signed and waymarked with its own distinctive logo: a white dragon-tailed seashell on a blue background surrounded by a yellow circlet bearing the words *'Llwybr Arfordir Cymru – Wales Coast Path'*. Look for the wood or metal fingerposts at main access points, in towns, on roadsides and lanes, and at key junctions.

Coastal Path fingerpost, Traeth Cymran, near Rhosneigr

Way to go: *Wooden signposts and waymarkers with the Wales Coast Path symbol mark the route*

Elsewhere the route is clearly waymarked with plastic roundels fixed to stiles, gateposts, fences and walls. In many places the Wales Coast Path waymarkers sit alongside others for already established routes—such as the Isle of Anglesey Coastal Path or the Pembrokeshire Coast Path National Trail. In some areas these local waymarkers are still more in evidence than the official Wales Coast Path ones; and on some stretches, waymarking remains patchy.

Official route waymarkers   *Official alternative route waymarker*

Alternative routes

Two sorts of alternative route are described in the guides. The first are the **official alternative routes** that avoid remote or challenging sections; and more attractive routes that, for example, provide better views or get farther away from motor traffic.

The second are our own **unofficial alternative routes**. Many of these are beach routes below the high water mark that by their nature are not permanently available, and so do not qualify as part of the 'official route'. Others are alternative high level routes or simply 'better' or more attractive, in our opinion. Both the **official** and **unofficial alternative routes** are shown on the maps in this book as a broken orange highlight.

Detours

The directions also describe **detours** to places of interest that we think you won't want to miss. These are usually short, off the main Path, there-and-back routes, typically of no more than a kilometre or so in each direction. Suggested detours can take you to anything from a special pub, castle or church to a stunning view or waterfall. If you've got the time, they bring an extra dimension to the walk. Detours are shown as a blue broken highlight.

Temporary diversions

There may be occasional or seasonal temporary inland diversions. The reasons for them vary from land management and public safety: forestry work, cliff falls, landslips and floods, to wildlife conservation: protecting seal breeding sites, bird roosts and nesting sites, and so on. Details of the latest permanent and temporary diversions can be found on the official Wales Coast Path website under 'Route Changes'. See **www.walescoastpath.gov.uk**.

Tides and tide tables

As much as five percent of the Wales Coast Path runs along the foreshore, between mean high and low water. These sections are naturally affected by the tide. On the whole, the official Wales Coast Path avoids beaches and estuaries. However, beaches often provide time-honoured, direct and pleasant walking routes and are usually safely accessible, except for around 1½ hours either side of high tide. If the tide is in, or you're in any doubt, take the inland route instead.

Occasional streams and tidal creeks may also be crossed at low tide but be impassable at high water. So it is a good idea to carry tide tables with you and consult them before you set out each day. They are widely available for around £1 from coastal TICs, shops and newsagents.

Several websites also give accurate tidal predictions for locations around the UK, including downloadable five day predictions. Useful websites include: **www.bbc.co.uk/weather/coast_and_sea/tide_tables** and **www.easytide.ukho.gov.uk**.

Tidal sands: *The expanse of Red Wharf Bay, one of the many tidal sections of the coast path*

Safety advice

If you're new to long-distance walking, or in one of the remoter areas, please remember:

- Wear walking boots and warm, waterproof clothing.
- Take food and drink.
- Mobile signals are patchy along much of the Path; let someone know where you are heading and when you expect to arrive.
- If you decide to walk along a beach, always check tide tables.
- Stay on the path and away from cliff edges.
- Take extra care in windy and/or wet conditions.
- Always supervise children and dogs.
- Follow local signs and diversions.

Emergencies

In an emergency, call 999 or 112 and ask for the service you require: Ambulance, Police, Fire or Coastguard.

Tell them your location as accurately as possible (give an OS grid reference, if possible; and look for named landmarks), how many people are in your party, and the nature of the problem. The phone app **what3words** is useful to identify your exact position and is now used by most emergency services.

Remember, though, that mobile signals may be poor or absent in some areas. Some coastal car parks and main beach access points have emergency telephones. Coastal pubs and shops may also have phones you can ask to use in an emergency.

Who manages the Path?

The Wales Coast Path is co-ordinated at a national level by Natural Resources Wales and managed on the ground by the sixteen local authorities and two National Parks through which it passes.

Funding has come from the Welsh Government, the European Regional Development Fund and the local authorities themselves.

For more details, see: **http://naturalresourceswales.gov.uk**

The Best of Anglesey

The **Isle of Anglesey** can boast some of the finest and most varied coastal scenery in Britain. During a 125-mile/200 kilometre circuit of the island, you'll experience the dramatic Menai Strait, broad tidal estuaries, sandy bays separated by rocky headlands, and dramatic cliffs sheltering quiet coves. For much of the route, Snowdonia's mountains and the Llŷn Peninsula form a dramatic backdrop to the coastal views. Along the way you'll find prehistoric monuments, sea arches and caves, a medieval castle, lighthouses and a church in the sea, as well as a wealth of wildlife from grey seals and dolphins to little egrets, peregrines, terns and puffins.

Menai Suspension Bridge

Beaumaris Castle

Trwyn Du lighthouse, Penmon Point

Stranded hulk, Traeth Dulas

Point Lynas and its lighthouse

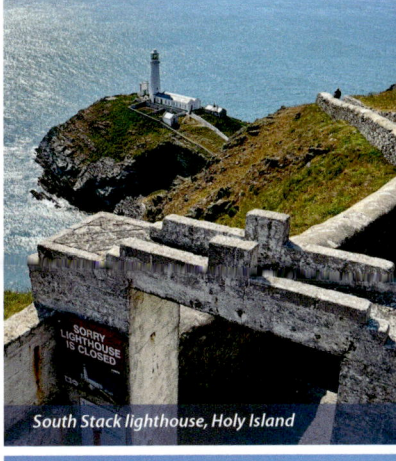
South Stack lighthouse, Holy Island

Bwa Gwyn sea arch, Rhoscolyn

St Cwyfan's Church, Porth Cwyfan

Llanddwyn Island, Newborough

Bryn Celli Ddu Neolithic burial chamber

The Isle of Anglesey
Part of the Wales Coast Path

Anglesey is Wales' largest island (approximately 48km/30 miles wide) and lies off the coast of North Wales. It is separated from the mainland by the Menai Strait—a narrow river-like channel 12½ miles (20 kilometres) long and just 250 metres wide at its narrowest point. Despite this, Anglesey is every bit an island and has a character very different to that of the mainland. Geologically it is an extension of the narrow coastal plain that fringes the mountains and is composed of flat or gently undulating farmland. The island's coastline, on the other hand, is both dramatic and varied, and those who visit the island with a view to exploring the coast will discover a stunningly beautiful landscape.

In fact Anglesey can boast some of the most varied coastal scenery in the British Isles. Within a ring of about 125 miles (200 kilometres) there are wide tidal estuaries, beautiful sandy bays, isolated coves, tiny villages and numerous off-shore rocks and islands. Anglesey also has one of the largest sand dune systems in the country, whilst other sections of the coast are as rugged and dramatic as anywhere in Britain and often far less crowded. Unsurprisingly, 85 square miles adjoining the coast has been designated as one of Wales' five Areas of Outstanding Natural Beauty (AONB).

A distant view of Ynys Llanddwyn and the Newborough dunes from Afon Cefni

The plan of the island is roughly square and each of its four sides has a very different character. The south coast, for the most part, borders the Menai Strait and, being sheltered from the open sea, shows few signs of the coastal erosion so apparent elsewhere. It is almost Cheshire-like with its green fields, hedgerows and woods, which in places reach right down to the water's edge—an unusual sight on the Welsh coast.

This stretch reaches its end at Penmon and immediately things change, although shelter from the prevailing wind is apparent in the lack of wind-sculptured trees and stunted bushes so characteristic of the west. The broad sweep of Red Wharf Bay is the main feature of this coastline, along with a number of small village resorts like Benllech and Moelfre. From Point Lynas the coast swings west into the Atlantic gales and things change dramatically. Just two small villages cling to this battered coastline which has been fragmented into a scattering of off-shore islets.

The most dramatic cliff scenery is to be found on the west coast; both on the northwest tip of the island between Carmel Head and Church Bay, and on Holy Island at Gogarth and Rhoscolyn. On the southwest tip of the island lower elevations have resulted in substantial sand dune systems rather than cliff scenery—Aberffraw and Newborough Warren being the most notable. Newborough has one of the largest dune systems in the country and is now a national nature reserve.

Walking Isle of Anglesey Coast Path

The Isle of Anglesey section of the Wales Coast Path makes a complete circuit of the island from Menai Bridge—offering approximately 200 kilometres/125 miles of superb coastal walking.

This guide divides the path into twelve day-walk sections and the chart below gives you the start and end points of each section along with grid references and distances making it easier to plan you walk. Each Day Section starts and finishes at or close to somewhere attractive and accessible with good facilities.

You will also need to know if any sections involve tidal restrictions, or are affected by seasonal or periodic closures.

Day Section	Distance	Start	Finish
Day Section 1 Bangor to Beaumaris	7½ miles 12 km	Bangor SH 585 732	Beaumaris SH 608 762
Day Section 2 Beaumaris to Pentraeth	12½ miles 20 km	Beaumaris SH 608 762	Pentraeth SH 535 798
Day Section 3 Pentraeth to Moelfre	6 miles 10 km	Pentraeth SH 535 798	Moelfre SH 512 864
Day Section 4 Moelfre to Amlwch Port	12½ miles 20 km	Moelfre SH 512 864	Amlwch Port SH 449 932
Day Section 5 Amlwch Port to Cemaes	7½ miles 12 km	Amlwch Port SH 449 932	Cemaes SH 371 934
Day Section 6 Cemaes to Church Bay	10½ miles 17 km	Cemaes SH 371 934	Church Bay SH 301 892
Day Section 7 Church Bay to Holyhead	14 miles 22 km	Church Bay SH 301 892	Holyhead SH 247 826
Day Section 8 Holyhead to Trearddur	11½ miles 18 km	Holyhead SH 247 826	Trearddur SH 255 790
Day Section 9 Trearddur to Four-Mile Bridge	8¾ miles 14 km	Trearddur SH 255 790	Four-Mile Bridge SH 280 783

Isle of **Anglesey** 33

Day Section	Distance	Start	Finish
Day Section 10 Four-Mile Bridge to Aberffraw	13 miles 21 km	Four-Mile Bridge SH 280 783	Aberffraw SH 355 689
Day Section 11 Aberffraw to Newborough	12 miles 19.5 km	Aberffraw SH 355 689	Newborough SH 426 640
Day Section 12 Newborough to Menai Bridge	11½ miles 18.5 km	Newborough SH 426 640	Menai Bridge SH SH 537 715

Distance chart for key locations along the path

	Menai Bridge	Newborough	Llanddwyn Island	Aberffraw	Rhosneigr	Four-Mile Bridge	Rhoscolyn	Trearddur	South Stack	Holyhead	Church Bay	Cemlyn Bay	Cemaes	Bull Bay	Amlwch Port	Llaneilian	City Dulas	Moelfre	Benllech	Pentraeth	Penmon Point	Beaumaris	Menai Bridge	Bangor	
Miles	131	125	122	113	108	101	90	82	79	77	71	66	64	56	53	51	42	33	23	20	18	13	8	4	**Bangor**
	131	117	114	104	97	90	86	81	75	69	55	49	44	38	36	34	28	24	20	18	13	9	5		7	**Menai Bridge**
	126	113	109	99	92	85	81	76	72	65	50	44	39	33	31	29	23	19	15	13	8	4		8	12	**Beaumaris**
	122	108	105	95	88	81	76	72	65	60	46	39	35	28	26	24	19	14	11	8		7	15	20		**Penmon Point**
	114	100	97	87	80	73	69	64	57	52	38	31	26	18	18	16	13	11	6	3		13	20	28	29	**Pentraeth**
	111	97	94	84	77	70	65	61	54	49	35	28	24	16	16	14	10	5	3		4	18	25	33	37	**Benllech**
	108	94	91	81	74	67	62	58	51	46	32	25	20	14	12	10	5		5	10	23	30	38	53		**Moelfre**
	103	89	86	76	69	62	57	53	47	41	27	16	10	8	6		7	13	17	30	37	45	68			**City Dulas**
	97	84	81	70	63	56	52	48	41	36	22	15	10	4	2		9	16	22	26	39	46	54	82		**Llaneilian**
	95	82	79	68	61	54	50	45	39	34	20	10	8	2		3	12	20	25	29	43	50	58	86		**Amlwch Port**
	93	80	77	66	59	52	48	43	37	32	18	11	6		3	8	16	23	28	33	46	53	61	90		**Bull Bay**
	87	73	70	60	53	46	42	37	31	25	11	5		10	13	21	26	33	38	43	56	63	71	103		**Cemaes**
	83	69	66	56	49	42	37	33	26	21	7		7	17	20	25	33	40	46	50	63	70	78	107		**Cemlyn Bay**
	76	62	59	49	42	35	30	26	19	14		11	18	28	31	35	44	51	61	74	81	89	114			**Church Bay**
	62	48	45	35	28	21	16	12	5		23	34	41	51	54	57	66	74	79	84	97	104	112	124		**Holyhead**
	56	43	40	30	22	16	11	7		9	31	42	49	59	63	66	75	82	88	92	105	112	120	127		**South Stack**
	50	36	33	23	16	9	4		11	19	42	53	60	70	73	77	85	93	98	103	116	123	131	132		**Trearddur**
	46	32	29	19	12	5		7	17	26	49	59	67	77	80	83	92	100	105	109	123	130	138	146		**Rhoscolyn**
	41	27	24	14	7		8	14	25	33	56	67	74	84	88	91	100	107	113	117	130	137	145	162		**Four-Mile Bridge**
	34	20	17	7		11	19	26	36	45	67	78	86	96	99	102	111	119	124	128	141	149	156	174		**Rhosneigr**
	27	13	10		11	23	30	37	47	56	79	90	97	107	110	113	122	130	135	139	153	160	168	182		**Aberffraw**
	9	3		16	28	39	46	54	64	72	95	106	113	123	126	130	139	146	151	156	169	176	184	196		**Llanddwyn Island**
	6		5	21	33	44	51	58	69	77	100	111	118	128	131	135	144	151	156	161	174	181	189	201		**Newborough**
		22	27	43	55	66	73	80	91	99	122	133	140	150	153	157	166	173	178	183	196	203	211	210	Kilometres	**Menai Bridge**

Distances are approximate to the nearest mile/kilometre

Day Sections

1: Bangor to Beaumaris

Distance: 7½ miles/12 kilometres

Terrain: Mainly flat, uncomplicated but varied walking alongside the Menai Strait. Once across the Menai Suspension Bridge, elevated lanes above the coast lead to Beaumaris

Points of interest: Bangor Pier, Menai Suspension Bridge

Note: Pubs and cafés in Bangor, Menai Bridge and Beaumaris. Accommodation, pubs, cafés, takeaways and shops in Beaumaris.

2: Beaumaris to Pentraeth

Distance: 12 miles/20 kilometres

Terrain: Coastal walking along the Menai Strait between Beaumaris and Penmon Priory. Quiet lane to Penmon, with mainly inland walking on field paths to Red Wharf Bay. Interesting section along the head of tidal marshes at Red Wharf Bay with a board walk.

Points of interest: Beaumaris Castle, Penmon Priory and dovecote, Penmon, Puffin Island, Bwrdd Arthur (Iron Age hillfort) Red Wharf Bay.

Note: Seasonal café at Penmon. Accommodation, pub, café, takeaway and late shop in Pentraeth.

A view across the Menai Strait to Bangor Pier

3: Pentraeth to Moelfre

Distance: 6 miles/10 kilometres

Terrain: Marshy walking around the edge of Red Wharf Bay. Short inland section to Benllech then excellent coast path between Benllech and Moelfre.

Points of interest: Red Wharf Bay, Benllech.

Note: Pub on the beach at Red Wharf. Cafés and shops in Benllech. Accommodation, pub, café and takeaway in Moelfre.

4: Moelfre to Amlwch Port

Distance: 12½ miles/20 kilometres

Terrain: Good coast path to Traeth Dulas. Inland section around the Llys Dulas Estate, followed by wild section of coast path to Point Lynas. Rocky coast path between Point Lynas and Amlwch Port.

Points of interest: Moelfre, Seawatch Centre, Lifeboat Station, *'Royal Charter'* shipwreck monument and site. Traeth Dulas. Point Lynas Lighthouse. Industrial heritage at Amlwch Port.

Note: Pub en-route between Traeth Dulas and Llys Dulas. Pubs and takeaway at Port Amlwch. Accommodation, bank, pubs, cafés, takeaways and shops in Amlwch.

Heading for Point Lynas near Fresh Water Bay

Beautiful decay: *Walkers look down on the decaying remains of Porth Wen Brickworks*

5: Amlwch Port to Cemaes

Distance: 7½ miles/12 kilometres

Terrain: Short urban section to reach the coast, then good coast path along a section of rocky open coast.

Points of interest: Industrial heritage associated with the copper industry at Amlwch Port, old brickworks at Port Wen and Llanlliana, Llanbadrig's Church, Cemaes.

Note: Pubs at Cemaes. Accommodation, pubs, cafés, takeaways and shops in Cemaes.

6: Cemaes to Church Bay

Distance: 10½ miles/17 kilometres

Terrain: Low-level coast walking with diversion around Wylfa Head Power Station, followed by wild undeveloped coast to Carmel Head and on round to Church Bay. Seasonal closure in operation between Carmel Head and Ynys Fydlin.

Points of interest: Wylfa Head Power Station, Cemlyn Bay lagoon, causeway and Nature Reserve, The Skerries, site of numerous shipwrecks, Ynys Fydlin island and sea arch. **Note:** There are no services en-route.

Bird's eye view: *An aerial view of Holyhead harbour from Holyhead Mountain*

7: Church Bay to Holyhead

Distance: 14 miles/22 kilometres

Terrain: A section of both level and undulating walking along a series of coves and beaches connected by lanes and bridleways. Inland section around Valley followed by the Penrhos Coastal Park on the outskitrs of Holyhead. Short urban section into Holyhead.

Points of interest: Stanley Embankment, Penrhos Coastal Park, Holyhead, Saint Cybi's Church, Roman coastal fort in the centre of Holyhead.

Note: Accommodation, banks, pubs, cafés, takeaways and shops in Holyhead.

8: Holyhead to Trearddur

Distance: 11½ miles/18 kilometres

Terrain: Leaving Holyhead there is some lovely walking through the Breakwater Coastal Park followed by some of the most rugged walking on the entire path over Holyhead Mountain, passing the lighthouses at North Stack and South Stack. The open headland known as The Range is one of the

Isle of Anglesey

largest areas of lowland heath on the island and is indented with numerous small coves.

Points of interest: Breakwater Coastal Park, North Stack Lighthouse, Holyhead Mountain, South Stack Lighthouse and RSPB centre, Ellin's Tower RSPB hide, Irishmen's huts Iron Age hut circles.

Note: Seasonal café at South Stack RSPB centre. Pubs, café, shop and accommodation at Trearddur.

9: Trearddur to Four-Mile Bridge

Distance: 8¾ miles/14 kilometres

Terrain: A fine section of coast once the holiday developments on the outskirts of Trearddur are behind you. Rocky and indented with small coves, the cliffs become higher and more dramatic in the approach to Rhoscolyn Head. There are fine beaches at Rhoscolyn and Silver Bay, but the path heads inland beyond these to Four-Mile Bridge.

Points of interest: Sea arches of Bwa Du and Bwa Gwyn, numerous small coves, Saint Gwenfaen's Well, grand views from the old Coast guard Lookout on Rhoscolyn Head.

Note: Pub at Rhoscolyn. Camp site at Four-Mile Bridge.

Church in the sea: *Tiny St Cwyfan's Church sits on an island near Aberffraw*

10: Four-Mile Bridge to Aberffraw

Distance: 13 miles/21 kilometres

Terrain: An unusual start with a section beside the tidal channel separating Holy Island from Anglesey. A mix of farmland and tidal inlets. A long section or beach walking to reach Rhosneigr with plenty of shops and services at the mid point of the walk. The chambered cairn above Cable Bay, the tiny islanded church of St Cwyfan and stunning views in the approach to Aberffraw provide the highlights for this section.

Points of interest: Tidal estuary ('Inland Sea'), Rhosneigr, Barclodiad y Gawres chambered cairn, Saint Cwyfan's Church.

Note: Shops, pubs and cafés at Rhosneigr. Accommodation, small shop and pub in Aberffraw.

11: Aberffraw to Newborough

Distance: 12 miles/19.5 kilometres

Terrain: The stunning beaches and large dune systems at Aberffraw and Newborough provide the highlight of this section. Mainly inland walking with a beach option leading to the village of Malltraeth. The Newborough Forest provides a very different type of coastal walking with the option to visit Ynys Llanddwyn.

Isle of **Anglesey** 41

Points of interest: Stunning beaches at Aberffraw and Newborough, Newborough Forest, Ynys Llanddwyn, Newborough Warren Nature Reserve.

Note: Pub, takeaway and café in Malltraeth. Accommodation, shop, café and pub in Newborough.

12: Newborough to Menai Bridge

Distance: 11½ miles/18.5 kilometres

Terrain: From Newborough the route is mainly inland through farmland to the Menai Strait. The Menai Strait section is a mix of waterside and farmland walking. There is a long inland detour around Plas Newydd with the option to visit Bryn Celli Du restored burial mound.

Points of interest: Newborough Warren Nature Reserve, Menai Strait, Bryn Celli Du restored burial chamber, Stevenson's tubular railway bridge, Telford's suspension bridge.

Note: Cafés at Foel Farm and Anglesey Zoo near Brynsciencyn. Cafés, pubs, takeaway and accommodation at Llanfair PG and Menai Bridge.

Ancient ship wreck on the beach near Newborough

Limited for time? —Anglesey in a nutshell

If you have limited time to explore this section of the Wales Coast Path—perhaps a weekend, or even just a day—then these key parts of the path are unmissable.

For a superb one-day walk, the section between Holyhead and Trearddur (Day Section 8) is about as good as it gets. This section circuits the northern half of Holy Island with a convenient bus link back to Holyhead. Alternatively, for a superb two-day walk, the section between Amlwch and Church Bay is recommended. This takes in almost the entire rugged north coast of the island. A regular bus service links back to Amlwch.

Best day walk
Rugged sea cliffs and the highest point on the island
Holyhead to Trearddur: 11½ miles/18 kilometres
From Holyhead (Day Section 8), the path heads up towards Holyhead Mountain through the Breakwater Coastal Park. Magnificent cliff scenery and iconic lighthouse at South Stack, followed by lovely lowland heath at The Range Car parking in Holyhead, regular buses between Trearddur Bay and Holyhead.

Panoramic view from Holyhead Mountain

Best weekend walk
Wild rugged coastline with cliffs and coves
Amlwch to Church Bay: 18 miles/ 29 kilometres
Day One: From (Day Section 5), indented rocky coastal walk passing through Bull Bay and the remote Porth Wen with its ruined brickworks to Cemaes. Accommodation, pubs and services at Cemaes.

Day Two: From Cemaes (Day Section 6), the route crosses Cemlyn Bay before circling the wild north west tip of the island to finish at Church Bay. Note: part of this route is seasonal access (see p 119).

Car park at Port Amlwch and regular buses from Llanfaethlu to Amlwch.

Cemlyn Bay and lagoon

A brief history of Anglesey

Rich in prehistoric remains, the site of Rome's destruction of the Druids and the seat of Welsh resistance during the Middle Ages

Anglesey has a rich historic heritage with visible remains of settlement reaching as far back as the second millennium BC. In fact Anglesey and nearby Llŷn have some of the highest concentrations of prehistoric sites in the British Isles. The reason is two fold—its location and topography. The position of Anglesey, thrust out into the Irish Sea, placed it on what is thought to have been one of the main communication highways of the prehistoric period.

The topography of the island also made it attractive to early settlers. Mainly flat with a covering of glacial drift, it has rich fertile soil and contrasts dramatically with the mountainous mainland. The coastal fringe may have always been clear of the thick woodlands which originally covered the interior and it is around the coast that the majority of prehistoric sites are located.

The earliest remains are found in the form of chambered tombs. Originally covered by a mound of earth which has invariably been removed by the elements over the centuries, only the rocks used to form the inner chamber are visible today. These monuments are associated with the late Stone Age culture in Britain and examples can be seen near Moelfre and Rhosneigr (Barclodiad y Gawres). Visitors to the restored burial chamber at Bryn Celli Ddu near Llanddaniel Fab, can see the supposed original form of these monuments.

The next phase of settlement (Bronze Age) brought immigrants known as the 'Beaker' people to Anglesey toward the end of the second millennium BC. It was these tribes who raised the island's many standing stones, although their purpose eludes modern historians.

The restored Neolithic burial chamber at Bryn Celli Ddu near Llanedwin

By the fifth century BC Celtic tribes had begun to move into Britain and by the time of the Roman conquest, Anglesey had become the most important centre for the Celtic or 'old religion' in Europe. Taught by a class of priests or 'Druids', it seems to have been they who stirred up the greatest resistance to the Roman occupation. There seems little doubt that it was to stamp out this seat of spiritual resistance that the Roman leader Suetonius Paulinus set out to invade Anglesey in AD 61. With an army of over 10,000 he crossed the Menai Strait and in one easily won battle extinguished the old Celtic religion completely. The sacred groves were destroyed and the Druid priesthood wiped out.

It was the Celts who introduced the Iron Age culture to Britain and they are perhaps best known today for the many hill forts which can be seen all over the country. Anglesey is no exception with fine examples crowning the summits of Holyhead Mountain and Bwrdd Arthur. The most impressive remains from this period are to be found near the coast path at Din Lligwy near Moelfre. Here the visitor needs little imagination to visualise the settlement as it was; hut bases, doorways and enclosure walls are all clearly visible.

Surprisingly, the Roman occupation left few remains on Anglesey, which was probably controlled from the fort at Caernarfon (Segontium) on the mainland. The most notable are to be found at Holyhead, where the walls of a coastal fort still enclose Saint Cybi's church in the centre of Holyhead and the base of a lookout tower, known as 'Caer y Tŵr', stands inside the old hill fort on Holyhead Mountain.

Roman origins: *The remains of a small Roman fort still enclose St Cybi's Church, Holyhead*

If you stand on this summit today, you will get a fine view out to sea in all directions, but on a clear evening you will see out to the west the Wicklow Mountains of southern Ireland and it was from here, when the protective arm of Rome had been removed, that raiders came in the early post-Roman era. These invasions inevitably resulted in settlement and it may be significant that the hut circles on Holyhead Mountain are known today as 'Cytiau'r Gwyddelod' or the 'Irishmen's Huts'.

The Irish invasion became such a problem to the inhabitants, not only of Anglesey but also the whole of North Wales, that a powerful Celtic chieftain either came or was sent from a northern British kingdom in Strathclyde and devoted the rest of his life to ridding the land of these invaders. His name was Cunedda and it was in a last battle on Anglesey that the Irish were finally defeated and expelled from Wales in about AD 470.

Cunedda established himself at Aberffraw where he built a palace close to the site of the present day village. In doing this, he founded a dynasty which would rule North Wales for almost eight centuries and produce such notable rulers as Rhodri Mawr, Gruffydd ap Cynan, Owain Gwynedd, Llywelyn the Great and his grandson Llywelyn the Last, whose defeat by Edward I in 1282 brought a final end to Welsh independence.

The reign of Maelgwyn Gwynedd, a descendant of Cunedda's, saw the firm establishment of Christianity in Anglesey, with the founding of monasteries at Penmon and Holyhead. Although he is said to have been a wicked ruler, the land on which these monasteries were built was granted by Maelgwyn.

The rule of the Welsh princes is unfortunately a rather sad period, being marked more by treachery and tragedy than any great political advancement. The progress made by some of the most successful rulers was often destroyed by the infighting of their descendants. This was caused in part by the tradition of dividing a man's possessions equally between his sons following his death. The result was a much weaker kingdom, particularly if he had many sons which was usually the case. Thus, brothers frequently fought each other for their share of the kingdom and rivals were often eliminated or imprisoned. Others made alliances with former enemies outside Wales in a desperate bid to gain what they saw as their birthright. These divisions were quickly exploited by both Saxons and Normans and Wales was never able to defend itself with a united force.

During the early years of the ninth century a new menace presented itself; one that came to be feared throughout the British Isles and one that Anglesey was particularly vulnerable to—Viking raids. By this time the Vikings had formed colonies at Dublin and in the Isle of Man and from there they launched attacks all along the Welsh coast. The monasteries at Holyhead and Penmon were attacked in 961 and 971 and the palace at Aberffraw was partially destroyed in 968. The Vikings formed no permanent settlements on Anglesey, but a number of names remain as evidence of their passing; notably Priestholm (Puffin Island) and The Skerries off the northwestern tip of the island.

The Norman conquest had little impact on Anglesey initially, although an early raid by the Earl of Chester in 1090 led to the building of a motte and bailey castle at Aberlleiniog near Beaumaris. This was soon destroyed by the powerful Gruffydd ap Cynan and the Normans made little real progress against the Welsh for the next 100 years.

When the threat of Viking raids ceased towards the end of the eleventh century, a period of prosperity followed and with an increase in population, a programme of church building began. This was the first time churches had been built in stone and a number have survived in part, notably Hen Capel near Moelfre.

Stamp of authority: *One of Edward I's finest castles at Beaumaris*

It was also during this time that deforestation of the interior of the island was finally achieved, releasing rich fertile land for agriculture and earning Anglesey the name 'Môn, Mam Cymru'—*Anglesey, Mother of Wales*. This referred to the vast quantities of grain which were grown here during the Middle Ages, sufficient it was said, for the whole of Wales. During the wars of independence the importance of Anglesey's ability to feed Wales was realised and both King John and Edward I made attempts to take Anglesey. It was the eventual loss of Anglesey that finally brought Llywelyn the Great out of hiding in the highlands of Snowdonia to bargain with King John and ensured Edward's final victory against Llywelyn the Last in 1282.

Following his conquest of Wales, Edward embarked on a programme of castle building all along the North Wales coast, the ruins of which still stand. On Anglesey he built his last Welsh castle at Beaumaris in 1295 near the site of one of Llywelyn's courts.

Wales was now subject to the English crown and the title 'Prince of Wales' reserved for the king's eldest son. The wars of independence were over, although Owain Glyndŵr was to raise the Welsh banner briefly at the beginning of the fifteenth century.

Although Wales was never to see independence from the English crown again, it did produce one of the most influential ruling families ever to sit on the throne of England—the Tudors. The seat of this family was Plas Penmynydd between Llangefni and Menai Bridge here on Anglesey. Henry Tudor's claim to the throne came through his descent from Owain Tudor and his rather mysterious marriage in 1429 to Henry V's widow, Queen Catherine.

Anglesey's position in the Liverpool sea lane and its proximity to Ireland have produced a rich maritime history. By the seventeenth century, packet boats were regularly crossing to Ireland from Holyhead, providing a service which was to expand in the nineteenth century when Thomas Telford completed his London to Holyhead coach road (now the A5) and built the graceful suspension bridge over the Menai Strait in 1826.

Today, tourism plays a key role in the island's economy and with recent road improvements on the mainland cutting the travelling time from Merseyside and Greater Manchester, Anglesey has become a popular destination for weekend breaks and second holidays. Away from the coast however, agriculture still dominates, although the emphasis is now on cattle and dairy farming, with little or no sign of its once famous corn fields.

Wildlife on the Isle of Anglesey

Day by day, the **Wales Coast Path** passes through a succession of different wildlife habitats: tidal strait, clifftop, beach, saltmarsh, estuary, forest and dune system, each bringing the chance to spot something new. Add to that the ever-changing weather and the round of the seasons and no two days are the same. Almost all the Anglesey coast is a designated Area of Outstanding Natural Beauty and includes Wales' largest National Nature Reserve. Keep your eyes open, and you're likely to see everything from seals and dolphins to red squirrels, puffins, ravens and choughs—plus maritime wildflowers, seabirds and butterflies in abundance. It's a naturalist's delight.

Red squirrel

Bird's-foot trefoil and thrift

Pyramidal orchid

Chough

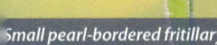

thrift or 'sea pinks'

Atlantic grey seal

Small pearl-bordered fritillary

Horned poppy

Sea holly

Sandwich tern

Red squirrels, orchids & choughs

Anglesey's varied coastal habitats mean walkers will discover a wealth of wildlife whatever the season

The **Isle of Anglesey** (or Ynys Mon, in Welsh) is rightly renowned for its varied and often beautiful coastline. Inland, the island's flat, fertile farmland meant it was often referred to as *Mam Cymru*, or the 'Mother of Wales', in the Middle Ages. Today, almost all the island's coast is designated an Area of Outstanding Natural Beauty, *"to protect the aesthetic appeal and variety of the island's coastal landscape and habitats from inappropriate development"*—making it the largest of the five AONBs in Wales.

The underlying geology is varied, too, with rocks dating from the Precambrian to the Carboniferous. Each of these rock types creates its own different habitat, which in turn supports specific types of wildlife.

What's more, and luckily for walkers, the Isle of Anglesey also enjoys its own microclimate. The island's separation from the mainland by the Menai Strait means it can often be grey and raining in Snowdonia while the sun shines steadily on Anglesey.

During its 125 mile/200 kilometre circuit of the island, the coast path passes through an exhilarating mixture of rocky strait, rolling farmland with pockets of woodland, open saltmarsh, mudflats and foreshore, vast sandy beaches

Newborough Forest and beach seen from Llanddwyn Island

and dune systems, coastal heath and forest, rugged cliffs and heather and gorse-clad headlands. This rich mix of habitats supports a wealth of wildlife from maritime spring flowers, orchids and butterflies to red squirrels, seals, porpoise and dolphins, terns, peregrines and choughs. Together, they'll enliven each day's walk around the coast.

Protected habitats

On top of its status as an Area of Outstanding Natural Beauty, many of Anglesey's coastal habitats have been given further UK and European protection. These include one National Nature Reserve, four Special Protection Areas, and twenty-six Sites of Special Scientic Interest (SSSIs). A further 31 miles of open, undeveloped coast around North Anglesey, Holyhead Mountain and Aberffraw are also protected as Heritage Coast. Together, they form some particularly beautiful and unspoilt sections where you can expect to see plants, animals and birds at every turn.

Around the island

The Isle of Anglesey is separated from mainland North Wales by the **Menai Strait**. Formed towards the end of the last Ice Age by rising sea levels flooding a geological fault that was later eroded deeper by ice, this narrow, 25 kilometre-long stretch of tidal water supports more than 1,400 species of plants and animals. This natural richness depends on the diversity of habitats in the Strait, rocky and scoured by violent currents in places, yet calm and muddy in others. Seaweeds flourish on the rocky shores, while the broad sand- and mudflats at either end of the Strait teem with marine invertebrates that attract feeding and roosting waders and wildfowl.

In contrast, the narrowest and fiercest section of the Strait between the two bridges, known as the **Swellies**, is home to unusual marine creatures such as sea anemones and sponges. The Strait is also used by seals and porpoises as a short cut between Caernarfon Bay and Liverpool Bay, with otters occasionally seen on the shore. It's a unique environment in the UK and there are plans to make it only the second Marine Nature Reserve in Wales

Marine fossils including brachiopods can be found in the Carboniferous limestone at **Penmon Point**, while the calcareous soils support an array of unusual plants including several orchids. Just offshore, uninhabited **Puffin Island** (also known as Priestholm or Ynys Seiriol) is a Special Protection Area for more than 750 pairs of breeding cormorants; it also hosts kittiwakes, guillemots and razorbills, as well as a few eider ducks and puffins.

Around the corner, the vast tidal inlet of **Red Wharf Bay** (Traeth Côch) covers more than ten square miles and supports huge numbers of waders and wildfowl, including redshank, knot, dunlin, curlew, oystercatcher and shelduck. Bordered by saltmarsh and sand dunes, its shell-rich shore hosts swathes of pyramidal orchids in summer.

Beyond Moelfre is the unspoilt enclosed estuary at **Dulas Bay** whose mudflats, saltmarsh and wild shores are good for breeding birds such as curlew, oystercatcher, shelduck, redshank, red-breasted merganser, ringed plover and little egret. Watch for peregrine, hen harrier and barn owl hunting the saltmarsh and reedy margins, too.

There are red squirrels in the woods at **Llys Dulas**. Anglesey's rocky eastern coast nearby is good for grey seals, porpoise and dolphins. The lighthouse

Curlews probe the tidal mudflats for invertebrates

Red beauty: *Anglesey's thriving red squirrels are a conservation success*

at **Point Lynas** attract early migrant birds, while the heathy headland here is excellent for seawatching for both harbour and bottlenose dolphins and porpoise in autumn and winter.

Beyond Amlwch, the rocky cliffs and headlands on Anglesey's **north coast** are great for nesting seabirds such as guillemots, razorbills and kittiwakes crowded onto the ledges. Choughs often feed on insects on the short clifftop turf, while gannets and peregrines pass nearby.

The curving shingle beach and lagoon at **Cemlyn Bay** support a large and internationally important nesting colony of common and Arctic terns, as well as one of the UK's largest breeding populations of Sandwich terns—featured on the logo for the Isle of Anglesey Coastal Path. Sea holly, sea kale, sea campion and yellow long horned poppies also thrive on the shingle ridge.

Offshore, a cluster of tiny rocky islets called the **Skerries** are home to more breeding Arctic and a few rare roseate terns. They also support gulls, kittiwakes and a few puffins.

Further round, Holyhead Island is home to the RSPB's iconic **South Stack** reserve. Situated high on heather and gorse-clad cliffs and with stunning panoramic views, their information centre at Ellin's Tower is complete with CCTV cameras. They overlook the busy nesting ledges below where you can

Living on the edge: *Kittiwakes breed on South Stacks' busy cliff ledges*

watch razorbills, guillemots and gulls from late March until July. There are puffins, too, and regular peregrine sightings. What's more, the rare South Stack fleawort is endemic here but it grows nowhere else in the world.

At **Aberffraw**, the vast dune system is a recognised SSSI and Special Area of Conservation that supports plants like sea holly, lady's bedstraw, marsh and pyramidal orchids, helleborines and creeping willow. The area is rich in invertebrates, too, and home to a variety of unusual birds such as breeding lapwing, skylark and chough.

A little farther south is the vast and empty **Malltraeth Bay**, once the home patch of renowned wildlife artist, CF Tunnicliffe. The open sands and **RSPB Malltraeth Marsh reserve** support a wealth of wildlife from breeding wetland birds including lapwing, redshank, curlew and snipe to overwintering bitterns, and a wide variety of waders and wildfowl. Smaller and rarer waders can often be found on the **Cob Pool**.

Beyond the Cob, the path enters lovely **Newborough Warren**. It's a vast marsh and dune-fringed area of forest, dune and open beach most of which is a National Nature Reserve. The saltmarsh bordering the forest here is good for hunting short-eared owl, hen harrier, peregrine and merlin in winter. But the forest's best known wildlife are probably the red squirrels whose numbers have risen steadily since their reintroduction in 1998, backed by a sustained, island-wide cull of the competing, non-native greys. Other animals found in the warren include frogs, toads, great crested newts, medicinal leeches, common lizards, grass snakes and adders, while up to 2,000 ravens roost in the heart of the forest on winter nights. The dunes and dune slacks are also rich in all sorts of rare and unusual plants, including butterwort, shore dock and dwarf adder's tongue. The huge numbers of orchids here include common-spotted, pyramidal, northern and early marsh orchids, common twayblades and the lovely dune helleborine.

Nearby is the iconic, fingerlike tidal **Llanddwyn Island** whose tiny offshore Ynys Adar (Bird Rock) supports 1% of the British breeding cormorant population. Watch for waders such as sandpiper oystercatcher and turnstone in the sandy coves and bays, with terns fishing just offshore in summer.

Beyond Newborough Warren, the path re-enters the **Menai Strait** whose mudflats teem with invertebrates, crabs and birds.

The varied landscapes along this section of the Wales Coast Path guarantees something new around every corner. There is sure to be something to delight nature lovers at any time of year, and it pays to have a good pocket field guide and pair of binoculars to hand.

Of course, this is no more than a brief summary of the wildlife you may encounter. For further details about the region's natural heritage, browse the Natural Resources Wales website at **www.naturalresourceswales.gov.uk.**

Coconut-scented gorse fringes the cliffs on Anglesey's rocky coasts

Day Sections

1. Bangor to Beaumaris *7½ miles/ 12 kilometres*
2. Beaumaris to Pentraeth *12½ miles/ 20 kilometres*
3. Pentraeth to Moelfre *6 miles/ 10 kilometres*
4. Moelfre to Amlwch *12½ miles/ 20 kilometres*
5. Amlwch to Cemaes *7½ miles/ 12 kilometres*
6. Cemaes to Church Bay *10½ miles/ 17 kilometres*
7. Church Bay to Holyhead *14 miles/ 22 kilometres*
8. Holyhead to Trearddur *11½ miles/ 18 kilometres*
9. Trearddur to Four-mile Bridge *8¾ miles/ 14 kilometres*
10. Four-mile Bridge to Aberffraw *13 miles/ 21 kilometres*
11. Aberffraw to Newborough *12 miles/ 19.5 kilometres*
12. Newborough to Menai Bridge *11½ miles/ 18.5 kilometres*

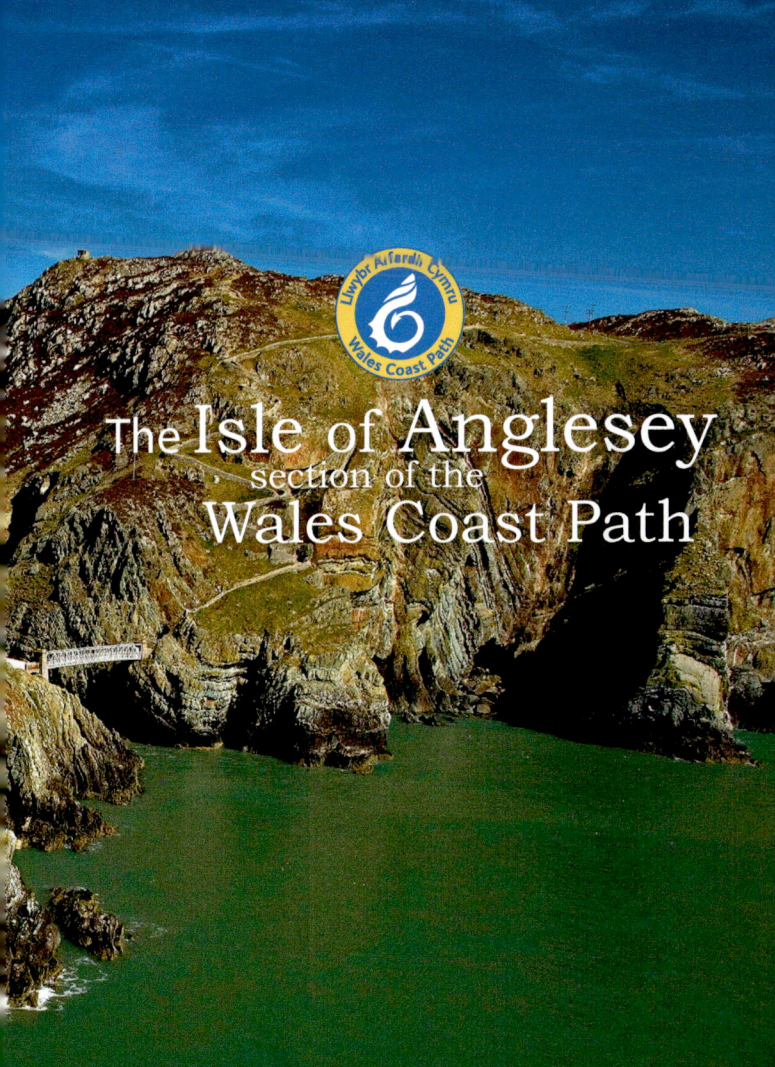

The Isle of Anglesey
section of the
Wales Coast Path

South Stack Lighthouse (Day Section 8)

Section one

Bangor to Beaumaris

Distance: *7½ miles/ 12 kilometres* | **Start:** *Bangor Pier, Bangor SH 585 732*
Finish: *Beaumaris SH 606 760* | **Maps:** *OS Landranger 115 Snowdon & Caernarfon*
OS Explorer 263 Anglesey East

Outline: A short, varied introduction to Anglesey alongside the tidal Menai Strait, crossing Telford's famous suspension bridge

The initial stretch along Menai's wooded shore ends with a crossing of the famous Menai Suspension Bridge, to reach the village of Menai Bridge, often described as the 'gateway to Anglesey'. An unavoidable section along the road is then exchanged for a quiet, elevated lane through Llandegfan with wide views across the Menai Strait back to Bangor and inland to the mountains of Snowdonia. The final few miles lead steeply down to the attractive town of Beaumaris.

Services: *Bangor is a busy university city with lots of accommodation, banks, post office, shops, pubs and bars, restaurants, cafés and takeaways. Cathedral, museum and pier. Public toilets by pier. Pubs, cafés, bank, cash machines, takeaway, Post Office and late shop en-route at Menai Bridge. Beaumaris has pubs cafés, cash machine and accommodation. Bus links back to Bangor.*

Don't miss: **Bangor Pier** – a classic Edwardian seaside pier | **Menai Suspension Bridge** – an engineering wonder of its day | **Beaumaris Castle** – One of Edward I's post-conquest fortresses

▲ *A view of the Menai Strait with Telford's iconic Menai Suspension Bridge*

Bangor

Bangor is a small coastal city on the Menai Strait overlooking the Isle of Anglesey. Centred on the ancient cathedral and university, the old city slopes in a maze of streets down to the pretty eastern end of the Menai Strait where refurbished Victorian Bangor Pier reaches out towards Anglesey. The view from the pier embraces the Great Orme, Llandudno, Snowdonia, Anglesey and, looking westwards along the Strait, Telford's iconic suspension bridge. It is an ideal place to start this lovely section of the Wales Coast Path, completing a circuit of the island of Anglesey.

Bangor takes its name from the old Welsh word for the wattle fence that enclosed early Christian sites. The Celtic Christian Saint Deiniol founded a monastery here in AD 550, and the present cathedral was built on the same site between 1496 and 1532. Throughout the Middle Ages, the cathedral was a spiritual centre for the independent principality of Gwynedd, and the tomb of the Welsh resistance fighter, Owain Gwynedd, can still be seen inside today. So it's no surprise that Bangor was the gathering point for medieval pilgrims starting out on the arduous journey to Ynys Enlli, or Bardsey, the 'island of 20,000 saints' at the very tip of Llŷn.

Bangor and its pier, backed by the mountains of Snowdonia

Strait and narrow: *Looking down the Menai Strait to the Britannia Bridge at low tide*

The route: **Bangor to Beaumaris**

1 This section begins at **Bangor Pier**, near **Garth**, at Bangor's most northern point. Here, the cast iron and timber Bangor Pier reaches almost halfway across the **Menai Strait** towards Anglesey's wooded shores.

Be sure to walk out onto 👁 Bangor Pier, whose onion domes, ornate shelters and pier-end tearoom all evoke Bangor's Edwardian hey-day as a seaside resort. There's a small fee, ample parking and toilets nearby.

From the pier, return to the corner opposite the pub above, and turn right, gently uphill on the quiet coast road. Within 500 metres, it narrows to a one-way section with adjacent cycle path. To continue on the main **official route**, walk ahead (to the left) on the gently rising road.

> **Alternative route**: *A pretty low-tide short cut along the Menai shore*
> Take the righthand fork here and drop down the narrow, tree-shaded lane to a boatyard. Turn left past sheds and moored boats. The path skirts the isolated **Old Bath House** to continue easily along the rocky shore for 500 metres to a large white house on the water's edge.

The **official route** continues uphill on the quiet road, veering away from the shore above a meadow with a **modern stone circle**. A few hundred metres later, the path kinks through a gap in the wall to follow a tarmac path along the upper edge of the field. Beyond the field, go right along the pavement for 400 metres, then turn right down signposted **Gorad Road**. At the bottom of the slope, cross the road, bear right, and head down the shaded lane ahead. The tarmac lane drops steeply beneath trees to emerge above a shingly beach.

Immediately above the shore, turn left and go through the signposted wooden footgate. Follow the field edge uphill to the right above the **white waterside house**. Keep to the field edge as it curves around to the left, to go through the wooden foot gate in the far, top righthand corner of the field.

For the next ½ mile/1 kilometre or so, the path runs through the lovely, ancient mixed woodland of the North Wales Wildlife Trust's '**Nant Porth Nature Reserve**'. The undulating path traverses the dappled slopes with occasional glimpses of the Strait below. Ignore faint paths down to the water, eventually climbing timber-edged steps to a ruined barn and kissing gate into fields at the top of the woods.

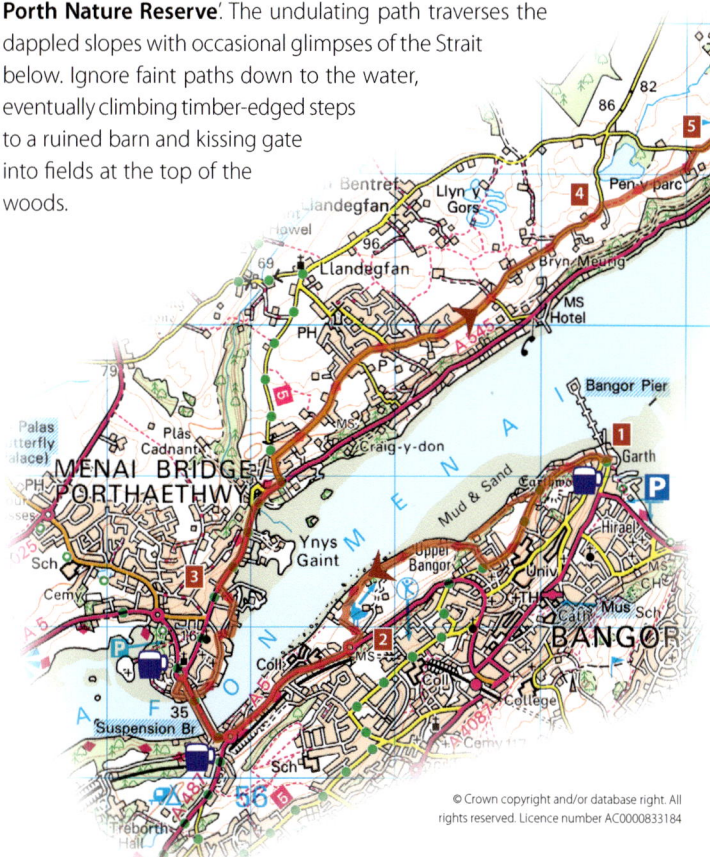

Wonder of the age: *Thomas Telford's iconic suspension bridge at Menai Bridge*

From here, a fenced path zig-zags around the periphery of several pastures to emerge at a metal kissing gate onto a tarmaced drive. Turn left and then right onto a narrow lane to emerge at a roundabout on the **A5** beside the entrance to **Bangor City Football Club**.

2 From the roundabout, turn right along the pavement beside the **A5**, signposted to 'Menai Bridge'. The path heads gently downhill past **Bangor University** grounds for just under ½ mile/1 kilometre to a large roundabout. Bear right here and cross the road opposite '**The Antelope' pub**, and turn right to the foot of Thomas Telford's impressive 👁 **Menai Suspension Bridge**.

Cross the bridge high above the **Menai Strait**. On the far side, cross to the left-hand side of the road and turn left immediately before the '**Anglesey Arms**' and following '**Beach Road**' down towards the base of the bridge. The road takes you under the huge buttresses of the **Menai Suspension Bridge**. Follow the lane through the quiet streets of **Menai Bridge**, past the slipway at **Porth y Wrach**, and turn right in front of the '**Liverpool Arms**' (Keep ahead to access the town centre facilities).

Where the road turns left, go straight ahead on to the **promenade** and swing left towards the **St Georges Pier**. Leaving the promenade turn right along the road. Carry straight on, ignoring 'Ffordd y Coley' (Askew Street) on the left, and then bear to the left to follow the main thoroughfare past the chapel to reach the **main road**.

3 Turn right along the road and follow it out of Menai Bridge. Cross the bridge over the tidal creek of **Afon Cadnant** with the islands of Ynys Gaint and Ynys Castell to your right.

Why so high?

The fame of Thomas Telford's iconic suspension bridge is well deserved. Completed in 1826 to carry his new coach road from London to Holyhead and ultimately Ireland, it was the largest span of any suspension bridge in the World at the time. It took eight years to build and was one of the engineering wonders of the age. The height of the bridge—over 100 feet—was required to allow sailing ships using the Menai Strait as a shortcut to pass beneath.

The Menai Suspension Bridge was the largest suspension bridge in the world

Bridging the gap

Reaching Anglesey

For centuries, reaching Anglesey from the mainland was a hazardous business. Despite being just 250 metres wide at its narrowest, the Menai Strait proved to be an effective barrier. A number of ferries crossed the Strait, but currents are tricky and numerous boats capsized or ran aground, with frequent loss of life.

With the Act of Union in 1800, Ireland joined the UK and the number of people crossing the Strait increased as politicians commuted between Ireland and London.

The route from London to Holyhead became an important highway, but the journey was notoriously slow and dangerous. In 1819, Thomas Telford (1757-1843) began working on ambitious improvements to the road. One of the biggest problems he faced in North Wales was bridging the Menai Strait. Telford was one of the finest engineers of his day and came up with a ground-breaking solution—the Menai Suspension Bridge.

Completed on 30 January 1826, the Menai Bridge was a triumph of civil engineering—the largest suspension bridge in the world at the time. Sixteen huge chains held up 579 feet of deck, allowing 100 feet of clear space beneath. It was rightly renowned as one of the wonders of the age.

More information: ww.menaibridges.co.uk

About 200 metres beyond the bridge turn left up a lane signed 'Llandegfan'. After a steep rise the lane swings right and levels. This gives relief from the traffic on the busy main road and although further from the coast, amply rewards the walker with extensive views to the Menai Strait and the mountains of Snowdonia.

After **Llandegfan** the lane becomes narrower with high hedges for about 1.6 kilometres/1 mile.

4 At the first major left-hand bend the coastal path leaves the lane to pass through the fields on the right (although during the winter it is less muddy to follow the lane).

A finger post and stone stile indicate the start of the path. Cross the stile, turn left for a few steps, then go ahead across the field at first, before following the footpath along a wooded bank to a kissing gate. Through the gate, head along a **boardwalk** then turn half-left through the field to a second kissing gate in the far wall.

Go through the kissing gate and follow a good footpath that weaves gently up through **scrubby woodland** to reach a third kissing gate in the fence near a large house—**Pen y Parc**. Go through the kissing gate in the fence and across grass to reach the driveway. Bear left down the drive and keep right where the drive forks to reach the lane.

5 Turn right and follow the lane, known as '**Allt Goch Bach**', past the **golf club** and down into **Beaumaris** with a fine view over the town and harbour. At the bottom of the hill turn right to reach the main road (A545). Turn left along the sea front into the town.

👁 **Beaumaris Castle** can be visited at the far side of the town.

Section two

Beaumaris to Pentraeth

Distance: *12½ miles / 20 kilometres* | **Start:** *Beaumaris Pier SH 608 762*
Finish: *Pentraeth SH 535 798* | **Maps:** *Ordnance Survey Explorer 263 Anglesey East, Landranger 114*

Outline: A long, mixed section along the coast to Penmon, then mainly inland paths with a final leg along Red Wharf Bay

From Beaumaris, the approach to Penmon is a mix of quiet lanes and foreshore with wide views across the Lafan Sands to Snowdonia. Penmon is Anglesey's eastern tip and the end of the Menai Strait and there is a noticeable change in the landscape once it is behind you. Heading inland, field paths and lanes climb to the limestone plateau of Bwrdd Arthur with its Iron Age fort and wide views. This is followed by a gradual descent back to the coast on the shores of the massive Red Wharf Bay. Easy walking to complete the day section with tidal implications in the final few miles.

Services: *There are pubs, takeaways, toilets and shops in Beaumaris, but very little for the rest of the walk except a seasonal café (Pilot House Café) at Penmon. Pub, Spar shop, takeways, WC and accommodation at Pentraeth. Bus links back to Beaumaris.*

👁 Don't miss: Castell Lleiniog – Early Norman motte and bailey castle | Penmon Priory and dovecote – atmospheric medieval priory

▲ *Penmon Lighthouse and Puffin Island*

Beaumaris

Beaumaris and its castle were built by Edward I following his conquest of Wales after a long struggle with the Welsh princes in the late thirteenth century. The name is thought to be derived from the Old French *beau mareys* meaning the 'beautiful marsh'. The land on which the castle and the town stands today, was originally part of the Menai Strait and ships could dock alongside the castle walls when it was first built—a common feature of Edward's castles. Much of the present town was built on reclaimed marshland, as the name suggests. The setting no doubt was, and still, is beautiful—backed by the rich farmland of Anglesey with wide views across the Menai Strait to the mountains of Snowdonia.

Beaumaris was the last of Edward's Welsh castles, built in response to the unsuccessful rising of Madog ap Llywelyn. Its construction covered a period of 30 years and it was never completed. It did however, see action in the Glyndŵr rising of the early fifteenth century and during the English Civil War in the 1640s.

Throughout the Middle Ages Beaumaris flourished and became the commercial capital of North Wales. It enjoyed the protection of a new town wall following its destruction at the hands of Glyndŵr's rebels, although this has not survived. A flourishing sea trade developed and goods were brought here from all over Europe. It was also the main point of access to the island; the place where the coast road from Chester to Holyhead and the Irish packet boats crossed the Menai Strait after a treacherous traverse of the Lafan Sands from Penmaenmawr. Only when Telford built his new suspension bridge in 1826 did emphasis shift away from Beaumaris.

Beaumaris Castle and its spectacular views to Snowdonia

The route: Beaumaris to Pentraeth

1 Facing the pier with the **Bulkeley Hotel** behind you, turn left along the **promenade**. Almost immediately, head right down a path alongside the **lifeboat station**. At the shore turn left and follow the promenade to its end.

Go through a kissing gate in the wall here leading into fields and follow the path close to the crumbling cliff edge overlooking the **Menai Strait**.

This path gives fine views out over the Menai Strait to the mainland where the rounded slopes of the Carneddau rise behind the coastal towns of Llanfairfechan and Penmaenmawr. To the north-east the weathered limestone headlands of Penmon and the Great Orme reach out into the Irish Sea.

2 Shortly you join the road again. Continue ahead to the end of the bay and walk down onto the beach here where the road swings left away from the coast. The next section is tidal, so if the tide is low, or falling, it is quite safe to continue along the beach to **Aberlleiniog**.

As you approach Aberlleiniog there are some interesting formations in the cliffs which clearly show the layering and composition of the glacial drift which covers much of the island.

Alternative route: *Inland option if tidal route is in doubt*
Stay on the road for another 1 kilometre and turn right at a crossroads following the lane for about 1.6 kilometres/1 mile to reach the coast again at Aberlleiniog where there is a small car park.

From the beach at **Aberlleiniog** bear left just before a stream (you can continue along the shore by fording the stream) to reach the lane.

Beaumaris

Section 2: **Beaumaris** to **Pentraeth** 71

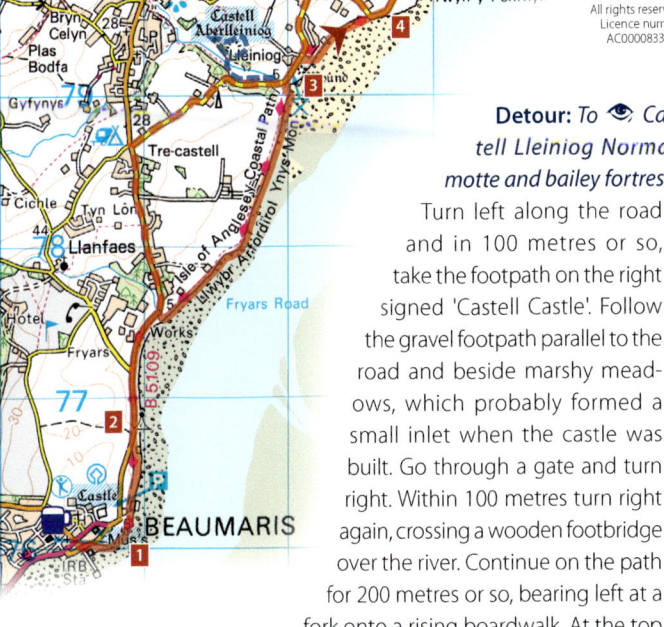

Detour: *To 👁 Castell Lleiniog Norman motte and bailey fortress*
Turn left along the road and in 100 metres or so, take the footpath on the right signed 'Castell Castle'. Follow the gravel footpath parallel to the road and beside marshy meadows, which probably formed a small inlet when the castle was built. Go through a gate and turn right. Within 100 metres turn right again, crossing a wooden footbridge over the river. Continue on the path for 200 metres or so, bearing left at a fork onto a rising boardwalk. At the top of the rise a signed footpath directs you right to the castle entrance. A path also circles the site giving a good impression of the remains.

Castell Lleiniog is a Norman motte and bailey castle originally built in 1090 by Hugh de Avranches, Earl of Chester. Both the mound and the moat are clearly visible. It was established during an early Norman advance into Anglesey but was quickly captured and destroyed by Gruffydd ap Cynan three years later. This swift action kept the Normans out of Gwynedd for the next 100 years. The ruins visible today are from the late Norman period; the original castle would have been constructed from timber.

3 Turn right along the road, passing the entrance to a **car park** and in a little over 200 metres, beside a house on the right, bear right down a wooded path. Go down steps onto the shore again and turn left along the beach. Continue to the large **concrete embankment** at the end of the small bay.

Alternative route: *Inland option if tidal route is in doubt*
This section is also subject to tidal restrictions. If in doubt continue along the road keeping right at a bend to reach Trwyn y Penrhyn.

Eastern limit: *Penmon and Puffin Island mark the eastern tip of Anglesey*

4 Join the lane again at **Trwyn y Penrhyn**, turn right and follow the lane to 👁 **Penmon Priory**.

The existing priory buildings date from the latter half of the twelfth century and housed a community of Augustinian monks until the Dissolution when the lands were granted to the Bulkeley family. The abbey foundation is much older and is traditionally associated with the monastery of Saint Seiriol, a contemporary of Saint Cybi who lived on Holy Island and the founder of a similar abbey there in the sixth century. The monastery that Seiriol established suffered badly in the late tenth century when there were repeated attacks from Viking raiders all along this coast. Two carved stone crosses from this period can be seen inside the church.

After the Dissolution of the monasteries in the sixteenth century the land and buildings passed into the ownership of the Bulkeley family who established the nearby deer park and built the dovecot around 1600.

From the Priory, a toll road leads down to the end of the headland at **Trwyn-du** (meaning 'black point'). There is no fee for those on foot.

At the end of the road there is a car park, and a small **café** with customers' toilets, open during the summer season. Just off-shore a tall black and white automatic lighthouse warns shipping of the dangerous sound between Anglesey's most easterly headland and **Puffin Island**.

Puffin Island is a haven for sea birds and can be reached by boat from Beaumaris. Its Welsh name—Ynys Seiriol—recalls the founder of the monastic settlement at Penmon. A second monastic community lived on the island itself and a small monastery existed that was still very much in use during the Viking raids of the tenth century. 'Priestholm', another name for the island, dates from this time.

Fresh meat and eggs

One of the most intriguing remains at Penmon Priory is the early seventeenth century dovecote This impressive little building was built by Richard Bulkeley, who acquired the abbey and its lands after the Dissolution, to house over 1,000 birds. They would have provided an important source of fresh meat. Eggs were collected by means of a ladder supported on the central stone pillar some twelve feet high.

The ruins that can be seen on the island today are the remains of a twelfth century church that replaced earlier buildings once the threat of Viking raids ceased. The only other building is a small nineteenth century semaphore station—part of a chain that extended all along the coast from Holyhead to Liverpool. It could transmit a message from Holyhead to Liverpool in just a few minutes.

There is no true coastal path between here and the National Trust land at Fedw Fawr. Paths and lanes inland must be used instead. Efforts are being made to try and improve the coastal path here.

5 From **Penmon Point** head back towards the **Pilot House Café** and bear right to follow a good path through an area of scrub to eventually emerge on Dinmor Quarry access road. Turn right and in around 30 metres, turn left through a kissing gate and walk ahead through a large field keeping to the right-hand side. In the field corner bear right through a kissing gate and keep beside the **old stone wall** on your left.

6 Go through a kissing gate at the head of the field, bear left and stay beside the wall again.

At the far end enter a narrow lane by a **small cottage** on the right and walk along the lane for about 500 metres to the first junction. Go straight ahead here and after about 300 metres turn right down a drive signed for the coastal path. Pass a group of houses and immediately before the last house, a little further on, turn left through an iron kissing gate onto an enclosed footpath which shortly leads into a field. Keep ahead by the left-hand

© Crown copyright and/or database right. All rights reserved. Licence number AC0000833184

Eastern tip: *Penmon Lighthouse and Puffin Island*

field edge and then follow an enclosed path to emerge beside a cottage at '**Cerrig Duon**'. Turn left on the access road for a few metres and then right through a kissing gate. Go ahead through a small field and look for an iron gate in the top corner.

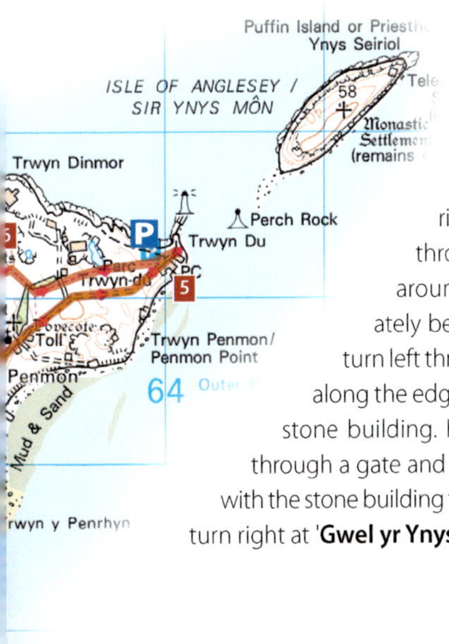

Keep ahead in the following field and join an access track beside a **small cottage**. Go ahead along the rough access road and after a short rise, where the track curves left, bear right on a broad, signed footpath through an area of gorse. Keep right around a large garden and immediately before a large, high, wooden gate, turn left through an iron gate and keep right along the edge of a large garden beside a high stone building. In the corner of the garden go through a gate and along an enclosed footpath, still with the stone building to the right. At the end of the path turn right at '**Gwel yr Ynys**' down a short drive to the lane.

Bear half-right here to where an iron kissing gate opposite leads into fields again. A fenced footpath heads down the field to where stone steps lead over the wall onto a track. Turn left along the track and follow it to a lane (ignore a right fork).

7 Turn right and walk along the lane to a T-junction (500 metres). Turn right here up the hill and follow the lane again for about 500 metres/¼mile.

8 Turn right through the kissing gate and head down the drive to '**Gwelfor**'. In a few metres bear right beside the hedge and through a kissing gate to the right of the farmhouse. Go through a gate onto the **National Trust land** at '**Fedw Fawr**'. **Stone slabs** take the footpath across a wet area beside a stream to soon emerge in an area of open heath and scrub.

Keep ahead (towards the sea) following the occasional waymarker posts and descending gently. At a T junction with a broader footpath where the trees begin to thicken, turn right for a few metres (car park directly ahead), then left as signed. Curve leftwards now beneath young trees to pick up the coast path along the seaward edge of a large, open, bracken and heather covered field.

There are good coastal views now looking back to Puffin Island and the distant Great Orme.

After a kissing gate, keep ahead close to the fence in another large rough grazing field. The worn trail is visible and easy to follow through the open fields and is marked by the now familiar yellow topped posts.

After **flat stone slabs** by a **stream** crossing, the path rises to pass through a more open grazing field. Go through a kissing gate in the corner, down steps and along the field

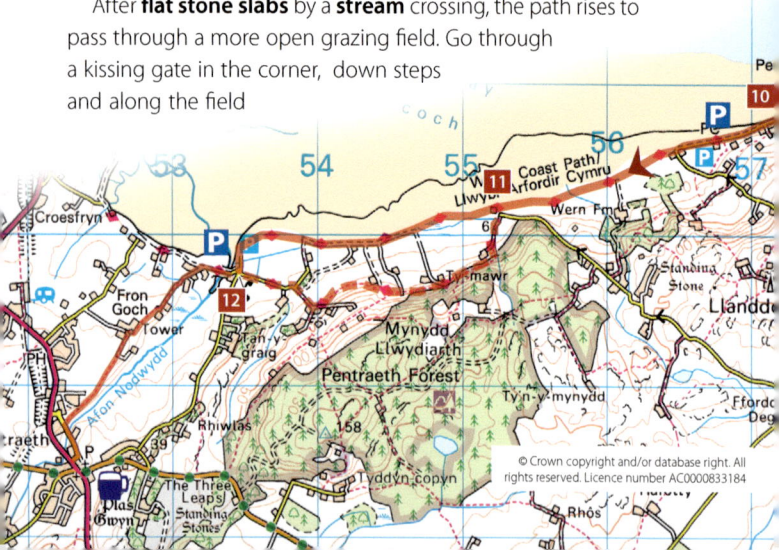

Grand view: *Looking out across Red Wharf Bay*

edge. Pass through an area of scrub, through a kissing gate followed by more scrub where a wide trail is now cut. At the far side of another grazing field, look for a marker post where **steps** climb up a wooded bank. At the top of the rise, bear right and follow the visible trail through another field of open gorse and bracken. Keep to the left of a **small stone ruin** and drop to a kissing gate leading down the bank into a green grassy field.

Keep to the right-hand edge of the field to reach a kissing gate in the far corner (ignore a gate on the right about 50 metres before the corner). Pass through another large field and through the kissing gate in the far corner. In around 50 metres or so, turn right towards a **small cottage**. Go through the gate and turn left along the unsurfaced access road.

9 At the signed coastal path in about 200 metres, turn right down a series of **steps** through scrub woods to a **kissing gate** with a view out across the bay (photo above). Through the kissing gate, go left on a clear path through more scrub woods to emerge in a field. Turn right along the field edge and go through a kissing gate in the bottom corner. Follow the clear-cut path across a bracken-covered bank and over a **sleeper bridge**. Continue on the path cut through more scrub and through a kissing gate onto an access track.

Turn right along the track. Almost at the end there is a small cottage ahead—'**Godreddi Mawr**'—and a narrow gate on the left immediately in front. Go through the gate and bear half-right across a field of scrub to the right of a bungalow, into more grazing fields. Go ahead keeping to the right to pass along the right-hand edge of the fields overlooking the rocky shore. Continue to where a kissing gate and steps before cottages, lead down onto the rocky beach.

10 Down the steps, turn left along the **beach** and cross a **stream** by a **footbridge** to reach the road by the coastal footpath sign. Turn right along the road which backs the beach.

Soon after a **car park**, where there is seasonal snack bar, the road bears left inland. Bear right (ahead) on the bend, leaving the lane to shortly cross a small **footbridge**. Follow the path ahead behind the **sand dunes** and along the edge of a large area of salt marsh. **Board walks** carry the path over wet and marshy sections.

At steps on the left, go up onto a **large stone-built seawall**. This is 500 metres/¼ mile long and gives a good, raised view across the salt marsh meadows.

11 After the sea wall, pass the entrance to a lane on the left. If the tide is high you may wish to follow the **alternative route** outlined below, which runs below **Pentraeth Forest** rather than walk the beach, but there is rarely any issue with this section even at high tide.

The **official route** continues ahead at the head of the salt marsh to reach the tidal parking area at **Pentraeth beach** where this section ends. This should be perfectly safe to walk other than during very high tides.

Alternative route: *Inland option if tidal route is in doubt*
Turn left off the beach along a sandy track to reach the lane. Turn right here up the drive to **Coch-y-Mieri farm**. Before you reach the farm, a

Crossing the footbridge at the eastern end of Red Wharf Bay

Board walk: *Looking back along the salt marsh margins at Red Wharf Bay*

signed path leads off left, going around a field below woodland. The path leads behind the farm and outbuildings to a fork. Ignore the left leading up through the woods turning right over a ladder stile. Follow the path through the trees with occasional fields to the right.

As you approach a large gate with a house beyond, bear left continuing through woods with fields to the right here and there.

Go through a kissing gate into woods and follow a gently rising path. Before you reach a kissing gate, bear right at a fork. This path soon curves right down to join an access track. Turn left along the track.

Follow the track to a junction by two houses and bear right. At a tarmac lane turn left and follow the lane to T-junction where a right turn leads down to the **car park at Pentraeth beach** to join the official route.

To finish this section at Pentraeth (just 1.6 kilometres/1 mile off the coast path) follow the lane over the bridge from the beach car park, then right over a second bridge crossing **Afon Nodwydd** (left if you followed the inland route). Walk along a sandy track to reach a couple of houses at **Pen-y-Lôn** by the entrance to a track. Turn left up the track (immediately before 'Pen-y-Lôn') and follow the public path to come out onto a lane in the village. Turn left up to a car park and the bus stop on the main road.

Section three

Pentraeth to Moelfre

Distance: 6 miles/ 10 kilometres | **Start:** Pentraeth beach SH 535 798
Finish: Moelfre SH 512 864 | **Maps:** Ordnance Survey Explorer 263, Landranger 114

Outline: A tidal estuary, holiday developments and one of the island's most popular resorts as well as two fine beaches

This section, although short and fairly easy, offers a lot of variety. Starting at the marshy southern edge of Red Wharf Bay, the path makes its way around the bay to the hamlet of Red Wharf Bay and the resort of Benllech. Beyond Benllech the path rises to run along a series of dramatic limestone cliffs on good paths sheltered by the thick hedges that bound much of the cliff-line. At Traeth Bychan you drop to the shoreline again, and continue at a low level to the attractive village of Moelfre.

Services: *The is an excellent seafront pub at Red Wharf Bay and in the large caravan park. En-route in Benllech there are public toilets as well as cafés and shops just off the path. Pub, cafe and takeaway as well as accommodation in Moelfre. Bus links back to Pentraeth from Moelfre.*

👁 **Don't miss:** **Ship Inn, Red Wharf Bay** – traditional pub in a lovely sea front location | **Traeth Bychan** – small beach where the submarine *Thetis* was brought ashore

▲ *Red Wharf Bay*

Red Wharf Bay

Red Wharf Bay is one of the largest expanses of sand on Anglesey. At low tide almost 10 square miles of sand and shallow channels are exposed, which attracts an abundance or wildlife, including large numbers of wading birds such as oystercatchers, purple sandpipers, curlew and dunlin.

The bay is bordered by salt marshes and small sand dunes rich in shell fragments that support wildflowers common to lime-rich areas including the pyramidal orchid.

The Welsh name for the Bay is Traeth Côch—the 'red beach', presumably from the rich colour of the sand. Despite its size, Red Wharf Bay has very little good beach sand—the edges of the bay are marshy rather than sandy—and has thus remained relatively undeveloped, in contrast to the adjacent Benllech. The walk around the bay is fascinating if a little wet in places. The pub and restaurants at the hamlet of Red Wharf Bay are situated in a lovely location enjoying wide views out over the sand and wooded hills and make a great start to this fairly short day section.

Looking across Red Wharf Bay to the Ship Inn

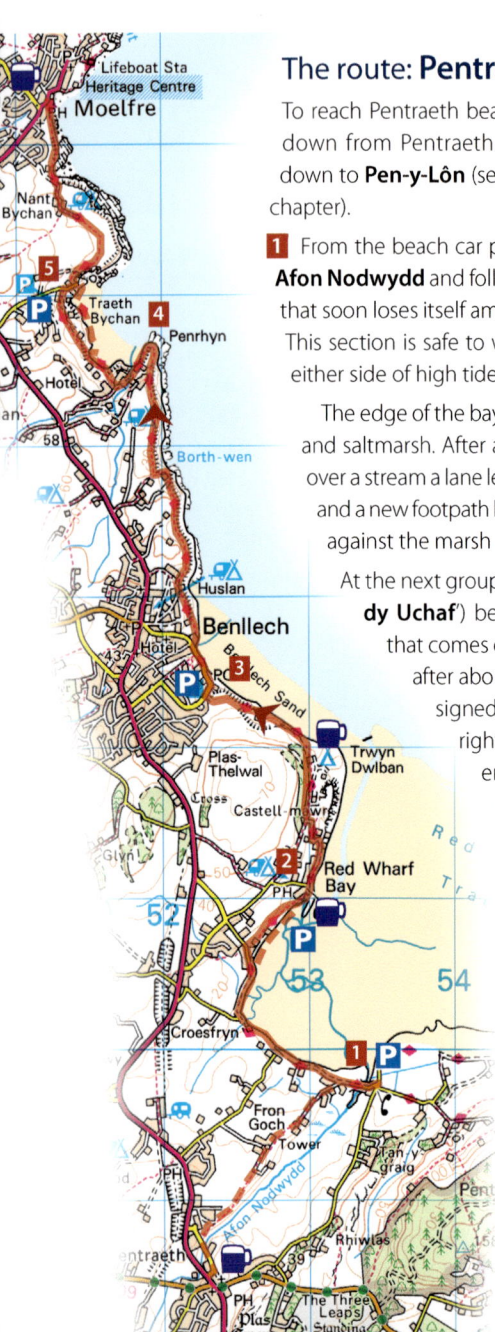

The route: **Pentraeth to Moelfre**

To reach Pentraeth beach either follow the lane down from Pentraeth or reverse the footpath down to **Pen-y-Lôn** (see the end of the previous chapter).

1 From the beach car park cross the bridge over **Afon Nodwydd** and follow the **tidal access track** that soon loses itself amongst the sandy marshes. This section is safe to walk apart from one hour either side of high tide.

The edge of the bay is a mixture of sand, mud and saltmarsh. After a small **stone footbridge** over a stream a lane leads down onto the marsh and a new footpath has been constructed tight against the marsh edge.

At the next group of houses ('**Porth Llông-dy Uchaf**') bear left up a tarmac road that comes down onto the marsh and after about 100 metres, look for the signed coastal footpath on the right (kissing gate). Follow this enclosed footpath along a wooded bank above the marsh to emerge in Red Wharf Bay beside the **Ship Inn**.

Alternative route:
Along the shore to the Ship Inn
At most states of the tide, the muddy shore can be walked from Porth Lôngdy Uchaf to Red Wharf Bay and the Ship Inn.

© Crown copyright and/or database right. All rights reserved. Licence number AC0000833184

Sea front pub: *Enjoying food and drink at the popular Ship Inn, Red Wharf Bay*

From here you have a fine view across the tidal sands of Red Wharf Bay, arguably one of the most attractive bays on Anglesey. Geologically it is the eastern counterpart of the Cefni estuary with just five miles separating the two. Unlike Red Wharf Bay, the sands of Afon Cefni have been extensively reclaimed so that the estuary today is a fraction of its former size. Originally Red Wharf Bay and Afon Cefni almost divided Anglesey into two separate islands.

One of the most attractive features of Red Wharf Bay and one which is quite rare on Anglesey is its background of hills—the wooded Mynydd Llwydiarth and the limestone plateau of Bwrdd Arthur. Both rise to over 150 metres/500 feet and stand guard over the southern arm of the bay isolating its eastern shore. Woods are also a feature of this locality. Elsewhere on the island deforestation since the Middle Ages has left the landscape bare with grazing and winter gales making the regeneration of woodland almost impossible.

2 Walk past the **Ship Inn** and continue along the road parallel to the beach. Ignore the drive to **Traeth Coch Sailing Club** on the left and continue along the driveway to a large house ('**Seagarth**'). Adjacent to the house, bear sharp left (almost back on yourself) onto a rising path. The path soon turns right beside a **caravan site** to emerge on one of the site roads.

Turn left into the caravan site and at the main site access road turn right.

Idyllic scene: *The popular beach and resort of Benllech*

After about 25 metres bear left onto the signed coastal path. Follow the path parallel to the site road and at the access drive to '**The View**' bear left up the drive. In about 35 metres, bear right as signed onto a path below a wooded bank. This passes behind the **clubhouse** and **The Tavern on the Beach** (public bar and restaurant). The path weaves in and out of the trees close to cliffs on the left to emerge above the beach.

Follow a raised concrete footpath beside a water treatment works on the left. Follow this to reach the road. Turn right down the hill into **Benllech**.

Benllech is one of the most popular beach resorts on the island and is busy throughout the summer. Cafés and gift shops selling ice cream and other seaside ephemera decorate the short sea front and give it a 'traditional seaside' feel. The centre of the village lies back from the sea front straddling the A5025—indicating that it didn't start life as a fishing village like nearby Moelfre. Development spread down the hillside towards the beach as its popularity grew in the early twentieth century.

The name Benllech means 'head of the rock' from the words 'pen' and 'llech', possibly a reference to the nearby sea cliffs. These cliffs are unusual for their thick vegetation and undergrowth. This is one of the few sections of east facing coast-

line in Wales and the difference between here and the more exposed coastline along the north and west of the island is immediately obvious.

3 Walk along the **waterfront** and take the signed coastal path on the right opposite '**Ffordd Cynlas**' road. The raised path crosses flat rocks in front of a **café** on the left before rising onto the sea cliffs overlooking the bay. The path is well-used and easily followed.

Sheltered coast

Most of the Welsh coastline is west-facing and exposed to the prevailing westerly winds. This produces an open landscape with low vegetation and few, if any, trees. Anglesey has the largest section of east-facing coast in the whole of Wales. Sheltered from the most severe winds, the landscape here is very different, with lush vegetation, trees and shrubs comparable with those found much further south.

Lush coastline: *The unusual limestone sea cliffs between Benllech and Traeth Bychan*

These cliffs rise to almost thirty metres in places and the path passes quite close to the edge so care is needed. Further along the coast are fine examples of wave-cut platforms; these take the form of flat rock ledges exposed at low tide. They are formed by wave erosion removing the upper rock layers and are particularly common where sedimentary rocks have horizontal layering. Other examples can be seen at the eastern end of Red Wharf Bay.

The path is well maintained and for most of the way is bordered by thick vegetation with only occasional glimpses of the cliffs below. Beyond the caravans ignore a footpath on the left, keeping ahead. Carry on along the path to the end of the little headland known as **Penrhyn**, which looks out over the bay at 👁 **Traeth Bychan** ('little beach'). There is a small cottage here.

Here you have a good view north across the bay of Traeth Bychan to the village of Moelfre. Traeth Bychan was where the submarine 'Thetis'—which sank with the loss of over 99 lives in 1933—was brought ashore after being raised from the seabed.

4 Follow the path around the headland and continue along the grassy path past several small **holiday chalets**. Join a tarmac access road heading down to a T-junction with a slipway on the right. Turn left up the hill and at the top of a short rise bear right (ahead) onto an enclosed signed footpath with **caravans** to the left. A gate at the end of the path takes you onto a drive with a **house** to the right. Immediately after the house, turn right as signed down the drive and where this curves right go ahead down the field towards the **beach**. Turn left along the beach.

Partway along the beach, at the end of the shingle, the coast path heads up into fields that back the bay. Follow the path ahead through three fields to a kissing gate on the right. Go through this and down **steps** into woodland to emerge in the beach car park. There is a small **café/shop** here open during the summer. Turn right out of the car park along the lane towards the beach.

Alternative route: *Along the beach if the tide is low*
If the tide allows you can walk along the beach to reach this point.

5 Turn left through a gate just before the beach, signed for the coast path. Keep to the right up the field, go through a kissing gate and follow the field boundary on your left through two fields to join an enclosed path.

The path eventually enters a farmyard at **Nant Bychan Farm**. Bear right along the farm access road and keep a look out for the coastal path sign on the right, which directs you down to the little shingle bay at **Porth yr Aber**. Turn left along the cove and follow the cliff path to **Moelfre**.

At Moelfre turn right down the hill into the centre of the village.

Following the coast path near Borth-wen

Section four

Moelfre to Amlwch Port

Distance: *12½ miles/20km* | **Start:** *Moelfre SH 512 864* | **Finish:** *Amlwch Port SH 449 932* | **Maps:** *Ordnance Survey* Explorer 263, Landranger 114

Outline: A long and fairly strenuous section along the rocky coastline punctuated by small coves and the beautiful beach of Traeth Lligwy

The section from Moelfre to the Dulas estuary is fairly flat and interspersed with the beautiful beaches of Traeth Lligwy and Traeth yr Ora, as well as the unusual tidal estuary of Traeth Dulas. Beyond Dulas the path follows a remote and undeveloped stretch of coastline diverting inland briefly around the Llysdulas Estate before heading north to Point Lynas. After the rocky cove of Porth Eilian low heather-clad cliffs are followed to reach the narrow harbour of Amlwch Port.

Services: *Moelfre has one or two shops, pub, B&B accommodation, camping and public toilets. Beyond Moelfre there is a seasonal beach shop/bar at Traeth Lligwy and a pub: The Pilot Boat before the Dulas Estate at Brynrefail. Pubs and fish and chip shop in Port Amlwch. Bus links back to Moelfre from Amlwch.*

👁 **Don't miss:** Seawatch Centre, Moelfre – lifeboat display and information on the *'Royal Charter'* shipwreck | **Royal Charter memorial** – site of the famous nineteenth century shipwreck | **Point Lynas Lighthouse** – dramatic lighthouse setting, good for dolphin watching.

▲ *The lighthouse at Point Lynas*

Moelfre

Moelfre is one the most attractive coastal villages on this side of the island. The tiny sea front and pebble beach is south facing and protected by a headland to the north. The prevailing westerlies, even on a blustery day, have largely exhausted themselves by the time they reach this part of the island and visitors can often enjoy warm, early spring, or late autumn sunshine here. The small size of the village does mean that it will be busy in the holiday season and there is little room for parking.

In the centre of the village you will see a large metal anchor on the right. This was taken from the wreck of the *'Hindlea'* which hit rocks nearby on 27 October 1959, almost 100 years to the day after one of the most famous shipping disasters of the nineteenth century happened in the same location —the sinking of the *'Royal Charter' (For the full story, see pages 92-93 below)*. So despite its sheltered location, Moelfre has become closely associated with two of the most famous wrecks around Anglesey's coast. There is a lifeboat exhibition in the Seawatch Centre and a statue memorial to Coxswain Richard Evans, who led many rescues around Anglesey.

The memorial to Coxswain Richard Evans at the Seawatch Centre, Moelfre

Fishing village: *Moelfre is a former fishing village with a sheltered shingle beach*

The route: **Moelfre to Amlwch Port**

1 From the little sea front, follow the road as it rises and where it bends left away from the sea, turn right onto the signed, paved footpath which overlooks the bay. Pass the 👁 **Seawatch Centre**, the monument to coxwain Richard Evans and **Moelfre Lifeboat Station** and continue ahead to the little **shingle beach** opposite Ynys Moelfre with its colony of sea birds. Turn left here across a small shingle beach. At the end the shingle by a row of low cottages on the left, go ahead keeping close to the coast edge.

Continue until the path enters a small **caravan site**. Look for a kissing gate on the right which will take you down to the bay at **Porth Helaeth**.

Just after Porth Helaeth, look to your left where a small 👁 **stone memorial** commemorates the wreck in 1859 of the *'Royal Charter'*. It reads: "This stone commemorates the loss of the steam clipper *'Royal Charter'* which was wrecked on the rocks nearby during the hurricane of 26th October 1859 when over 400 persons perished. Erected by public subscription in 1935."

The memorial overlooks the bay where the ship was wrecked and can be approached by a short field path on the left.

The path continues along a series of low limestone cliffs passing two private cottages at **Porth Forllwyd**. Turn right now and continue to reach **Lligwy Bay** and beach car park.

2 Walk through the car park and a small area of sand dunes to cross the stream by a **wooden footbridge** and a smaller **stone footbridge**. Pass through a second car park and continue ahead along the coastal path.

The first small cove—**Porth y Môr**—is shingle. Drop down and walk along the beach, then continue to **Traeth yr Ora**, a beautifully secluded sandy cove which cannot be approached by road. The coast path cuts around the perimeter of an ideally situated campsite just the cove, exiting by a kissing gate on the right. Beach access is down steps to the right, otherwise continue ahead rising to a bench and kissing gate immediately above the beach. (You can continue ahead through the gate to follow a path to the end of the headland beyond Traeth yr Ora returning to this point to continue.)

A contemporary etching of the wreck of the Royal Charter

The 'Golden Wreck'

Just offshore is a Victorian 'treasure ship' wrecked in a hurricane in October 1859

Close to the coast path at Lligwy Bay during very low spring tides can be seen the twisted iron ribs of a once proud ship, the luxury clipper, *The Royal Charter*. She was returning from the Australian gold fields only to be wrecked close to her home port of Liverpool during a freak hurricane in October 1859. It was the worst storm of the century.

Her fate shocked the British Empire. The wreck claimed the lives of all but 39 of the 493 passengers and crew. No women or children survived. She also carried to the bottom a fabulous treasure: gold bullion in the form of bars and bags of gold dust and nuggets—insured to the contemporary value of £322,440—as well as another probable £150,000 in gold sovereigns belonging to

Australian natural gold nugget

her passengers. That valuation was based on a gold price of £4 an ounce; in modern terms, the cargo was worth closer to £80-100 million.

The Australian gold rush had begun at Ballarat in 1852 and thousands of Europeans and Americans flocked to Australia to seek their fortunes. Many were successful and booked return trips on the *Royal Charter*, an iron-hulled luxury clipper with an immense spread of sail and an auxiliary steam engine. She regularly completed the journey in under 60 days—two weeks faster than even her closest rival.

Two months after leaving Melbourne, the *Royal Charter* sighted Wales. But as dawn rose over the Irish Sea, the wind veered to the north.

A newspaper correspondent described the worsening weather: "*The wind gradually freshened during the afternoon ... till over the mountains came a thin black haze, which rose into the air with an ominous rapidity and overspread the sky.*" From a strong south-easterly gale at Force 9, the wind changed first to east-north-east at Force 10—and then to a full hurricane at Force 12.

The Royal Charter struck the rocks bow on and began to break up. The sea was a maelstrom of white water. A handful of people struggled ashore.

Joe Rodgers managed to get a rope ashore by climbing the cliffs and rescue at least a handful of those on board. His actions are celebrated in the memorial at the Seawatch Centre in Moelfre

But most either drowned huddled in the saloon or were pounded to death against the rocks. Bodies were washed ashore for weeks afterwards, and are buried in local churchyards.

Most of the bullion was recovered but of the estimated £150,000 in sovereigns, only £1,200 was officially surrendered to the Receiver of Wrecks. Having bravely saved a number of passengers, some of the locals also became illicitly rich overnight.

Today, a poignant memorial in nearby St Gallgo's churchyard commemorates the wreck and its victims.

> "At first sovereigns had drifted in with the sand and been scattered far and wide over the beach, like sea shells."
>
> All the Year Round, *Charles Dickens, 1859*

More information: For a very readable account of the wreck and its aftermath, see *The Golden Wreck: The Tragedy of the Royal Charter*, by Alexander McKee, 1986.

3 Otherwise, turn left on the official route which rises to **Penrhyn farm**. Turn right at the farm onto a rough access road. This shortly joins another access road where you should bear right and continue to a T junction with a tarmac lane. Bear half-right across the lane to a kissing gate into fields.

4 Walk ahead up the field keeping to the right of a **house and garden**. Through a kissing gate continue up the gently sloping fields. Near the top of the field look for a squat waymarker post on the left which directs you half-left through a **gap in the scrub bushes**. Follow the path up the bank then turn right between the fence and wall to emerge in a grazing field. Walk ahead now keeping to the left of a wooded rise and to the right of a large pool, to a kissing gate in the far left corner leading onto a farm track. Follow the track ahead for about 300 metres and where this bears right, a kissing gate directly ahead takes you into fields once more. Walk ahead along the right-hand field edge to the **Pilot Boat Inn**.

Part-way up the road towards Brynrefail (on the left) there is a monument in fields dedicated to the Morris brothers. These four brothers grew up at Pentre Eirianell just below the Pilot Boat Inn in the early eighteenth century. They became famous for the many thousands of letters they wrote to each other during their working lives which have remarkably survived and give a fascinating glimpse of life in rural Wales, particularly Anglesey, during that period. Lewis Morris, the eldest of the brothers, is also noted for his sea charts which were published in 1784.

Traeth Lligwy is one of Anglesey's fines stretches of sand

Ageing gracefully: *A picturesque hulk at Traeth Dulas*

5 Turn right down the road and look for the signed coastal path on the right in about 200 metres. This follows a farm access road. In about 250 metres turn left along a grass track which soon opens out into a small field. Bear right down the field and cross a **footbridge over the river**. Beyond the bridge walk ahead on a stone-paved path to pass between **two large stones** used as old gate pillars and turn right along the field edge. Go through gates, over a small footbridge and keep ahead through the next field crossing a larger footbridge to reach a lane. Turn right along the lane

6 The lane soon deteriorates into a rough **tidal road** running along the edge of the estuary. Parts of the tidal road will be submerged at high tide, but there is a rough path on the left above the usual tidal limit.

7 In about 600 metres, and immediately before the third house on the left, turn left up a tarmac lane which comes down onto the sand. Walk up the lane passing the **church of Saint Genllwyfo** on the left and then, just before the rectory on the left, take the signed coastal path on the right. Walk diagonally across a field to a kissing gate in the far corner to reach a lane.

8 Turn right along the lane passing '**Plas Uchaf**' and continuing past the wooded **Llysdulas** estate on the right. Watch out for red squirrels among the laneside trees. The lane eventually levels by **The Home Farm** on the left and a little further on there is a sharp left-hand bend with a track on the right

Rocky finger: *The crag-lined headland of Point Lynas and its lighthouse*

and a house—**Mulberry House**—ahead. The signed coastal path follows the access road ahead, to the right of the house. Where the road bends right, cross the ladder stile ahead into fields. Walk ahead through the following fields to reach the coast at **Porth yr Aber**.

Immediately ahead you can see the rocks of Ynys Dulas, which lie a mile (1.6 kilometres) offshore. The tower which can be seen, was built as a refuge for shipwrecked sailors in the last century and was kept stocked with food and provisions —an indication of the frequency of shipwrecks along this coast.

9 In the bottom corner of the final field, turn left, soon crossing a footbridge and kissing gate. Keep ahead along the right-hand field edge above the rocky coast. In the far corner go through a kissing gate, down the bank and follow the path through the small sloping field which backs the little cove of **Porth Helygen**. The path is fairly clear now and is marked by low waymarking posts.

10 The next cove—**Porth y Gwichaid**—is larger and has a shingle beach. The coastal path keeps to the left of steeper bracken-covered ground, then takes a direct line through the small fields that back the bay. As you begin to ascend, the path veers away from the coast edge and is marked by yellow-topped posts. At the top of the slope keep ahead on the path through more open rough ground. Soon **Point Lynas Lighthouse** comes into view ahead and the path cuts through bracken scrub to cross a footbridge above rocky **Fresh Water Bay**. Continue on the good path through more bracken and gorse to eventually enter open fields by a kissing gate (ignore a kissing gate up to the left just before this. Walk directly down the fields and after overhead cables, turn left through a kissing gate and go ahead to join the access road to the lighthouse.

Point Lynas Lighthouse

The long, finger-like headland of Point Lynas has posed a threat to Liverpool bound shipping for centuries. In 1766 a Pilot Station was founded here to guide ships into Liverpool but it was not until 1779 that the first beacon was built by the Liverpool Pilotage Service. The present lighthouse dates from 1835 and is unusual in having the lantern at ground level. The light, which flashes every ten seconds, can be seen for a distance of twenty miles. It is now automated.

Detour: To 👁 Point Lynas Lighthouse

A right turn here will take you to the lighthouse, but you will need to return to this point to continue the walk. A path circles the lighthouse to a viewpoint well-know locally for watching porpoise and other cetaceans.

11 Turn left and walk along the road to **Porth Eilian**.

Porth Eilian and the parish of Llaneilian derive their name from Saint Eilian who is said to have landed at nearby Porthyrychen with his cattle and possessions in the sixth century and established the first church here. According to local legend, he obtained the land for his church from Caswallon Law Hir (Caswallon The Long Handed), the king of Gwynedd at that time. Eilian is said to have struck the king with blindness for some misdemeanour. Caswallon was later forgiven, his sight restored and out of gratitude (or fear!) he promised Eilian a piece of land to establish his church. It was agreed that Eilian would have all the land crossed by a deer of his choice before being caught by Caswallon's dogs.

The chase started at Dulas and led towards Parys Mountain and Llam Carw (later known as 'Harts Leap'), here the hart escaped by plunging into the sea. Thus Eilian acquired enough land to build his church and establish the settlement of Llaneilian.

At Porth Eilian there is a turning area and a slipway onto the beach. A fingerpost ahead beside a driveway indicates the continuation of the coastal path which is well-walked and easily followed. The first section is cut through gorse scrub, then after a kissing gate the coast path heads through a large open field, with a short dip to **Porthyrychen**. After a rise and more open ground, there is a short descent to a **timber footbridge** across a stream. Look

© Crown copyright and/or database right. All rights reserved. Licence number AC0000833184

to your left where a large rock lies beside the stream and to the left of this, a second rock has a spring bubbling from beneath it. This is **Ffynnon Eilian**.

Ffynnon Eilian is said to be the holy well of Saint Eilian, although some pre-Christian beliefs are associated with it. It is said to have been used in the past as a cursing well, possibly connecting it to the story of Eilian and Cadwallon. Remnants of a dry-stone wall enclosing the well can still be seen at the foot of the large rock from which the water flows.

12 From Ffynnon Eilian the coast path continues ahead over open heath. It is well-used and easily followed. Keep right at a fork after a **footbridge** and in just over 1 kilometre/¾mile reach a larger inlet with a small house beyond. This is **Llam Carw**. Head towards the house.

Go through a kissing gate to the left of the house in the corner by the wall and keep ahead to a large **car park**. Follow the road beyond the car park, past a tower and in front of the entrance to the **Anglesey Marine Terminal**. Bear right down past the **Sail Loft Visitor Centre and Café** to emerge at the harbour at **Amlwch Port**. Walk left along the quay and bear right along a path at the back of the harbour. This leads to a slipway at the back of the Port where this section ends.

To reach Amlwch town centre you will need to walk away from the slipway down '**Quay Street**' and turn right past the **Liverpool Arms** pub. Go up the hill along '**Machine Street**' and then turn left along '**Lôn Goch**'. Turn right, cross the old railway and you will come out at the main bus stop opposite the supermarket [0.75 kilometre/½ mile].)

Looking back to Point Lynas Lighthouse

Section five

Amlwch Port to Cemaes

Distance: 7½ miles/ 12 kilometres | **Start:** *Amlwch Port SH 449 932*
Finish: *Cemaes SH 371 934* | **Maps:** *Ordnance Survey Explorer 262 Anglesey West & 263 Anglesey East, Landranger 114*

Outline: A superb section of the coast path. An impressive, rocky coastline with a visit to Wales' northern-most point

Once you are beyond immediate vicinity of Amlwch the coast is both wild and beautiful. A section over low rocky cliffs leads to the small village of Bull Bay with its handful of houses and tiny shingle bay. Beyond Bull Bay is the wide rocky mouth of Porth Wen with its deserted brick works and sea arch and a little further on is Llanlleiana Head, the northern-most tip of Wales. The dramatict coast continues to the little church of Llanbadrig, clinging to the sea cliffs and overlooking the sheltered bay at Cemaes.

Services: *Cemaes has pubs, takeaways and cafés as well as post office and a pharmacy. A regular bus service gives easy access back to Amlwch as well as on towards Holyhead. Accommodation at Cemaes. Bus links from Cemaes back to Amlwch.*

Don't miss: Porth Wen – wild, remote bay with derelict brickworks | Llanlliana Head – the most northly point in Wales | Llanbadrig – tiny ancient church on the cliffs overlooking Cemaes Bay

▲ *Looking ahead to Llanlliana Head above Porth Cynfor*

Amlwch

Amlwch owes its existence to the rich copper reserves to be found at nearby Parys Mountain. The Romans are thought to have mined copper here and it is almost certain that such rich reserves would not have gone unnoticed in prehistoric times. After the Romans there seems to have been little interest in copper or mining activity in the area until a sharp rise in the price of copper began in the late seventeenth century with an increase in the production of guns and its use as protection for the hulls of wooden ships.

Parys Mountain was one of the richest reserves in the country and in the latter half of the eighteenth century two local entrepreneurs, Sir Nicholas Bayly and Rev Edward Hughes developed the mines to their greatest extent. Some 1,500 people were employed and the mining companies were even minting their own coins. The local agriculture must have suffered badly as the higher wages offered by the mining companies drew workers off the land. Smelting industries were also developed here and as production from the mines reached 44,000 tons per year the town grew from a small village into a prosperous market town.

With so much hanging on the price of copper things were always going to be fickle and the turn of the nineteenth century saw the beginning of a decline in the industry. Throughout the early nineteenth century the price of copper continued to fall and the mines declined. They were no longer of any significance after the 1850s.

The strange landscape of Parys Mountain copper mines

Tranquil scene: *Bull Bay's Welsh name, Porth Llechog, means 'slaty port'*

The route: **Amlwch Port to Cemaes**

To reach the coastal path from the centre of Amlwch, leave the bus station and walk down the road crossing the old railway. At the T-junction turn left, signposted to 'Amlwch Port'. At the end of the road turn right, and at the 'Liverpool Arms' turn left down 'Quay Street'. Keep left at the slipway to join the coastal path [0.75 kilometre/½mile].

1 From the square by **The Adelphi** pub at **Amlwch Port** walk down towards the harbour, bearing left before the slipway as signed. Pass a small building and cross a **footbridge**. At a junction bear left to join a track. Here you have the option of turning right for a short detour to **Trwyn Penwaig** to view the harbour (you will need to return to this point to continue), otherwise turn left. In a few metres, keep left at a T-junction, then, in about 15 metres turn right through a car park and cross a **playing field**. At the far side of the field go through a kissing gate and turn left along the banks of the aptly named **Afon Gôch** ('red river') to a kissing gate at the road.

Turn right along the road for about 75 metres, then left through another gate. Cross the disused railway line and follow a gravel path ahead to a kissing gate. Go through the kissing gate and turn right along a track. Keep right (ahead) at a fork and at the end of the track go through a gate by '**Costog Fawr Cottage**'. Follow an enclosed path down to the sea.

2 The well-defined coastal path heads left along low cliffs for about 1.25km/1 mile to reach the main road. Turn right here and walk along the road into **Bull Bay**.

An information board in the car park partway along the road explains the origin of the English name for this village which is taken from the name of the nearby cove Porth y Tarw—tarw meaning 'bull'. A literal translation of Porthllechog would be the 'slaty port'. The board also carries information on the local flora and fauna, along with a brief mention of the ancient rocks in evidence here. These are pre-Cambrian, thought to be 570 million years old and some of the oldest rocks in the world.

3 Turn right down into the village by the '**Bull Bay**' sign. At the end of the tiny bay turn right immediately before cottages onto a narrow path between gardens with the bay to your right. Rise up concrete steps to a kissing gate and turn right along a short tarmac road to a turning area, then go over a stone stile. Follow the path around the headland—which is open grassland—through a kissing gate. The path ahead is straight forward now and follows the coast edge for about about 1.5 kilometres/1 mile.

As you round the headland of Trwynbychan you get a fine view into the wide, rocky bay of Porth Wen with its abandoned brickworks. With no real beach to absorb the impact of winter storms, the slaty rock has weathered into a series of jagged narrow inlets that cut in towards the footpath.

The remains of Porth Wen Brickworks can be seen across the bay. The works used quartzite to make silica bricks. The existence of quartzite here possibly gave the bay its name; Porth Wen means 'white port' and Craig Wen, from which the white crystal was taken, means 'white crag' or 'white rock'.

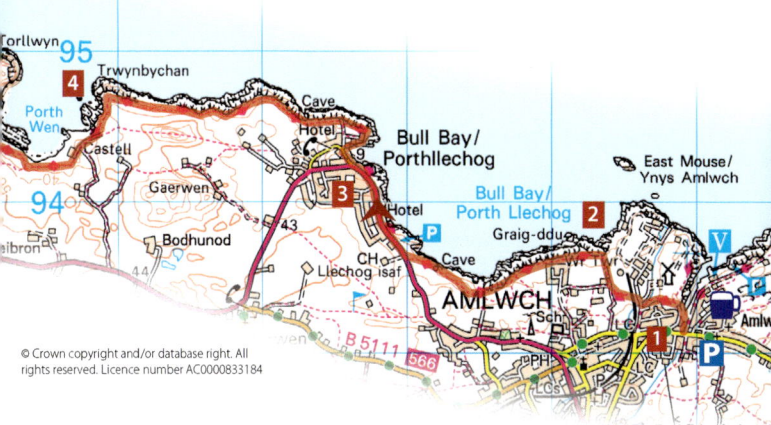

© Crown copyright and/or database right. All rights reserved. Licence number AC0000833184

Rocky bay: *The old brickworks at Porth Wen, one of the few large bays on the north coast of Anglesey*

4 Soon after the coast path swings left high above the wide, rocky bay of 👁 **Porth Wen**, it joins an enclosed farm track heading towards a stone farmhouse ('**Castell**'). Walk past the front of the house and over a stile in the wall. Head directly through the following field, up a gorse covered bank, through a kissing gate and continue ahead keeping slightly right. Beyond a sleeper bridge and kissing gate, bear right along a farm track which soon becomes a grassy footpath around the back of Porth Wen bay. Go through a kissing gate in the far corner and across the next field. Go through another kissing gate and rise to meet a track above the old brickworks. Turn right along the track. As you approach the headland of **Torllwyn** (mast) keep left at a fork.

Detour: *To Torllwyn viewpoint*
It is worth the short detour right through to Torllwyn for the wide views it allows of the coast in both directions.

Nearby are the white quartzite crags which were used by the brickworks. A little further on there is a fine view along the coast to Llanlleiana Head with the island of Ynys Badrig beyond.

5 A good path traverses the coastal slope which is quite high and steep here, then drops to a rocky inlet immediately before 👁 **Llanlleiana Head** at **Porth Cynfor**. Cross the stile and walk directly up the steep slope between two small rock outcrops. Higher up bear right a fork. (The path on the left leads directly to Porth Llanlleiana avoiding the climb and steep descent from Llanlleiana Head.) As you crest the hill, head for the lookout, a **ruined summerhouse** built by the Stanleys.

Porthwen Brickworks

On the west side of Porth Wen, you will see the abandoned Porth Wen Brickworks with its tall chimney and distinctive beehive shaped kilns. This enterprise used quartzite from nearby Craig Wen to make silica bricks for use in the steel industry. Silica brick helped maintain the high temperatures required for steel manufacture. The works operated from 1850 to 1914, then at a reduced level until it finally closed in 1949.

Decaying enterprise: *The ruined works at Porth Llanlleiana*

This headland is Wales' most northerly point and there is a fine view in both directions taking in almost the entire northern coast of Anglesey—from Point Lynas in the east to The Skerries beyond the northwestern tip of the island. The head is also topped by the remains of an Iron Age hillfort known as Dinas Gynfor

6 From the summerhouse the path swings back, then zig-zags down to **Porth Llanlleiana** and its ruined works. Opposite, go up steps steeply then continue on a grass path soon beside a wall on the left.

Eventually the path swings left up through two kissing gates and a set of timber steps and continues much the same until it swings left above a high rocky inlet to a kissing gate. Through the gate, the path heads right, soon beside little graveyard of 👁 **Llanbadrig Church**.

7 At the church follow the path around the cemetery, then bear left to the lane by the gate.

Alternative route: *Around the headland of Llanbadrig Point*
Follow the path around the headland and drop onto the shore at low tide to rejoin the main path south of Porth Padrig if you prefer.

The church is dedicated to Saint Patrick, who was sent to convert the Irish by Pope Celestine in the fifth century and reputedly stands on one of the oldest Christian sites in Wales, possibly dating from as early as AD 440. How Saint

Patrick came to build a church here is not clear but local legend maintains that he founded it in gratitude for his safe arrival ashore, after suffering shipwreck on nearby Ynys Badrig. Porth Badrig is the supposed location of his landing after which he found shelter in a nearby cave, now known as Ogof Badrig.

The present building is a small structure, just 20 metres by 4.5 metres and stands on the very edge of the cliffs, exposed to the frequent winter gales which sweep in from the Irish Sea. It is mainly of sixteenth century construction although sections of the interior may date from medieval times.

In 1884 it was restored by Lord Stanley of Alderley, whose work showed the influence of his recent conversion to the Muslim faith. Much of this was destroyed by fire in 1985, although recent renovation has allowed it to be open to the public once more.

The headland beyond the church (Llanbadrig Point), as well as south of Porth Padrig is owned and managed by the National Trust. It gives fine views of the bay.

Walk down the lane from the church passing the beach at **Porth Padrig** and turn right onto the coastal path enclosed by fences (the shore option rejoins here). This takes you around the headland of **Trwyn y Parc** and down to a lane. Turn right here, walk through the **car park**, along the **promenade** at the back of the bay, through **another car park** and then left up to the road. Turn right along the road and cross the **bridge** into the village of **Cemaes**.

© Crown copyright and/or database right. All rights reserved. Licence number AC0000833184

SECTION SIX

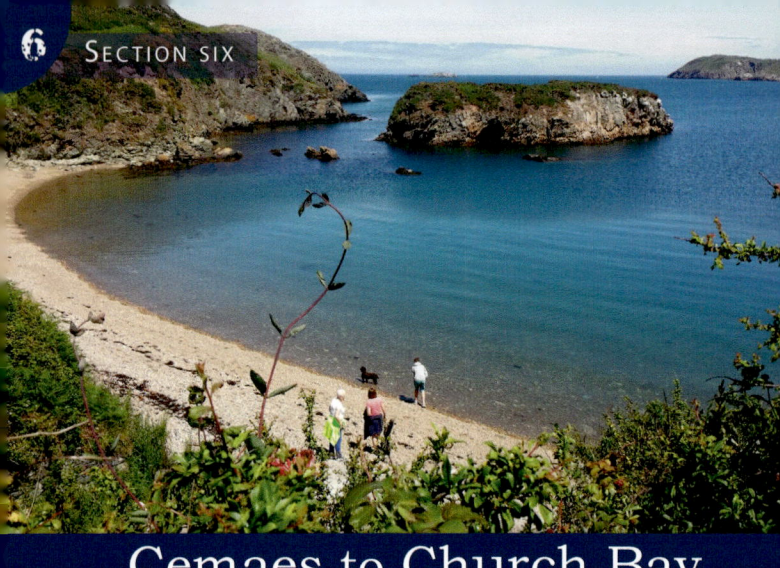

Cemaes to Church Bay

Distance: *17km/10½ miles* | **Start:** *Cemaes SH 371 934* | **Finish:** *Church Bay SH 301 892* | **Maps:** *Ordnance Survey Explorer 262, Landranger 114*

Outline: A long, varied and in places, remote section of the coast. A stark contrast between Wylfa Power Station and Carmel Head

This section explores the island's most remote section of coast around Carmel Head. Most of the land is owned by the National Trust and is remote and unspoilt. In dramatic contrast, Wylfa Nuclear Power Station sits between Cemaes and Carmel Head. Once Wylfa Power Station is behind you, however, a beautiful stretch of rocky coastline unfolds, with wide views out to The Skerries and across the bay to Holy Island. The high sea cliffs between Carmel Head and Church Bay are broken only by the tiny island of Ynys y Fydlyn with its dramatic sea arch and secluded cove.

The section of coast around Ynys y Fydlyn is only open between 1 February and 14 September. Outside these dates an inland option must be followed.

Services: *There are pubs, cafés, takeaways, a post office, cash point and a general store in Cemaes, as well as B&B accommodation. Nothing en-route, café bar/hotel and accommodation at Church Bay. Pub at Llanfaethlu along with bus links to Cemaes Bay and Valley/Holyhead.*

Don't miss: **Cemlyn Bay tern colony** – large breeding colony | **Cemlyn Bay Nature Reserve** – unusual causeway beach and lagoon

▲ *Secluded cove and Porth yr Ogof*

Cemaes

Cemaes originated as a fishing village and has the distinction of being Wales' most northerly settlement. Prior to the great road improvements of the nineteenth century, poor inland communication links meant that travel by sea was Cemaes only reliable link with the outside world. This led to the development of the small harbour which, by the early nineteenth century, consisted of a stone pier behind which fishing boats sheltered from frequent winter storms. In 1828 a particularly violent storm destroyed part of this structure and a new one was designed by Ishmael Jones, a local entrepreneur. This was complete by 1835 and a small ship building industry developed with vessels from 100 to 400 tons being built here.

Ships from Cemaes traded in coal, limestone, corn, marble, lime and ochre. An indication of Cemaes' commercial links with England can be seen by the fact that many public buildings in Liverpool are built from limestone and marble exported from Cemaes. The chimney of the old brickworks behind Cemaes can be seen from the main road. The harbour also benefited from the success of the nearby copper mines on Parys Mountain.

Cemaes' sea-trade began to decline in the mid-nineteenth century with the introduction of the railways and the improvement of the road system on the mainland. Today the village markets itself as a holiday resort. There is a fine, safe beach and the surrounding coastal scenery is amongst the best on the island.

Pleasure craft in the little harbour at Cemaes

The route: **Cemaes to Church Bay**

1 From the **centre of Cemaes** on 'Bridge Street' take the narrow street to the right of '**The Stag**' pub. This is the road that backs the **harbour**. Follow this and at the far end of the bay take the signed footpath on the right. Walk up a steep tarmac and gravel path and where this levels turn right onto a narrow footpath immediately after **Viking Cottage** on the right. At the end of the footpath there is an access road—turn left along this and go straight ahead where the road bends left. Follow the path along the coast.

Beyond the houses the path bends left to an access drive. Follow the signed footpath to the right here between **stone pillars** (immediately before the drive) and continue along the coast edge.

There is a fine view back to the village from the top of the rise and in clear conditions the peaks of Snowdonia can be seen on the skyline.

As you round the bay above **Porth Wylfa**, go through a kissing gate and walk along an enclosed footpath that backs the cove. Exit into a field at a kissing gate on the left after about 350 metres. Bear right across the field to a second kissing gate in the far hedge.

2 Ignoring the well-used path ahead (this can be used to by-pass Wylfa Head—see opposite page), turn right and follow the edge of the field along the coastal edge to **Porth yr Ogof** where there is a small boathouse down on the shore and a **rocky island** with a small cave. Stay with the path ahead and a little further on the path passes through **stone gate pillars** onto **Wylfa Head**.

© Crown copyright and/or database right. All rights reserved. Licence number AC0000833184

Bay watch?: *Lookout station on Wylfa Head*

The land at Wylfa Head was given to the public in 1969 by the Central Electricity Board to celebrate the investiture of Prince Charles.

3 Follow the path ahead through the gateway and out to the end of the head and bear left passing a small **lookout building**. Follow the path along the coast edge with the **nuclear power station** looming ahead. Go through a small gate beside a stile in a wall tight beside the **perimeter fence** and walk ahead through the field towards a pole carrying **overhead power lines**. Go through a gap in a wall between **stone gate pillars** and keep ahead along the right-hand field edge to a kissing gate in the fence on the right. Go through the gate and take the path ahead to join a track near **stone gate pillars**. Turn right to pass through a kissing gate beside the gate pillars.

Alternative route: *To cut out the circuit of Wylfa Head*
Walk directly across the large open field at **Point 2** with the roof of **Wylfa Power Station** peeping over the trees, into a copse. A path leads directly through the trees to a kissing gate to the right of a large **stone gate pillars**, originally part of Wylfa Hall, demolished in the 1960s.

There is a **car park** on the left here used by anglers and those walking on Wylfa Head. Opposite the car park entrance, turn right into the woods and follow the path through the trees. The footpath is gravel at first (ignore a right) before swings left up **wooden steps** to a T-junction—turn left here,

Storm beach: *The unusual shingle beach and brackish lagoon at Cemlyn Bay*

make a short rise, then descend a zig-zag path down more **wooden steps**. Pass beneath a large **pylon** keeping ahead through the woods.

4 Emerge from the trees and turn right to join the access road to the power station. Turn left along the road and follow it as it bends left heading for the site exit. In about 400 metres there is a crossing and you will see the signed Coastal Path directing you right. Go through the field gate. **The next section of the route may well change if plans for a new power station get the go ahead**. In the meantime follow the fenced path ahead beside the track with a **stone wall** to the right. The path crosses the track a few times, finally veering away right between fences.

Go through a kissing gate at the end of the path and walk directly across a field towards the right-hand edge of a **small conifer wood**. Drop down the bank into a tiny cove with the gardens of **Cestyll** to the left. Cross a **small stone footbridge** over the stream, pass the **ruined mill** on your left and follow the coastline rightwards onto the headland beyond.

5 The path stays outside walled fields on the left before curving left into the wide sweep of **Cemlyn Bay**. Go through the timber kissing gate and continue to the shingle beach and car park.

The unusual formation of this beach has been caused by centuries of onshore winds, depositing stones and shingle across the mouth of the bay to form a ridge ('esgair') of stones. This has created a brackish lagoon on the landward side fed by fresh water and inundated by the sea only on the highest tides. Water level in the lagoon is maintained by a weir at the far end of the beach.

The lagoon was managed as a private wildlife refuge for 40 years until the National Trust bought it with funds from Enterprise Neptune in 1971. It is now leased

Tern colony

Cemlyn beach is the breeding site one of the largest tern colonies in Britain and returns here each spring. The reserve provides a unique opportunity to view a tern colony at such close quarters, although you are requested to follow the viewing instructions so as not to disturb birds during the breeding season (April – August). Please do not walk along the ridge between April and July when the birds are nesting.

by North Wales Wildlife Trust who maintain it as a nature reserve. Unsurprisingly, the pool is a haven for wildlife and supports large numbers of grey mullet along with a variety of wildfowl including mallard, shelduck, redshank, oystercatcher, red-breasted merganser, coot, little grebe and tufted duck. Of particular note is the tern colony, one of the largest in Britain with birds returning each spring to breed.

Tidal note: Access at the far end of the shingle bar can be restricted by the tide, but only at high tide thanks to the **causeway**.

Alternative route: *High tide inland route*

For the high tide option, follow the lane out of the car park, turning right at the next three junctions around the back of the lagoon past '**Plas Cemlyn**' and into a car park. Go through the car park towards the headland of Trwyn Cemlyn.

Continue along the beach (**Esgair Cemlyn**) and at the far end cross the **stone causeway** over the outlet stream from the lagoon to reach an unsurfaced road and car park. Turn right and follow a track towards the headland of **Trwyn Cemlyn**.

Alternative route: *Around Trwyn Cemlyn*

If you have time it is worth the short walk around the headland of Trwyn Cemlyn for the view of the bay and the coastline ahead.

The tidal causeway at the western end of Cemlyn

Section 6: **Cemaes Bay to Church Bay**   115

Into the wild: *Heading towards Carmel Head on the coast path above Hen Borth*

6 Bear left following the wall to a corner overlooking flat, wave-cut rocks, where a kissing gate leads into fields on your left. The path now keeps tight against the right-hand field boundary, overlooking the sea to your right.

Follow the coastal path to the small shingle cove of **Hen Borth**.

7 From here the coastal path hugs the coast to **Carmel Head**—almost 3.5 kilometres/2 miles.

Northwest of Carmel Head lies the group of rocks known as The Skerries—a Norse name and one of the surprisingly few legacies from the Norse raids of over 1,000 years ago.

Other links with shipping can be seen in the two large beacons known as the 'White Ladies'. These line up with a similar tower on West Mouse and acted as a guide for shipping negotiating Carmel Head.

8 As you approach the tall stone towers known as the '**White Ladies**', the coastal path veers away from the coastal edge, passing to the right of the seaward tower. Cross a footbridge over a ditch and keep ahead passing a **tall chimney** associated with local mining.

> **Detour:** *Closure between 14 September and 1 February*
> If the Ynys y Fydlyn section is closed, you will need to head inland from here following a rough farm track to **Mynachdy farm**. Turn right at the

Lighthouse on the Skerries offshore islands

Rocks, reefs & shipwrecks

Dramatic offshore islands with a lighthouse and important seabird colonies

From Carmel Head and the surrounding coast at low tide there is a panorama of wave-cut rocks and small islands out towards The Skerries. The name comes from a Scottish diminuitive of the Old Norse word sker meaning a rocky offshore island. On a blustery day, there is a strong Hebridean feel to this remote weather-beaten corner of Anglesey, which stands in sharp contrast to the softer south and east coasts.

Lying on the busy Liverpool shipping lane, it has been a major hazard to shipping for centuries. This was particularly true during the age of sail, when numerous ships were driven onto its notorious reefs and islands by onshore winds. The area is also known for its strong currents.

Moelfre lifeboat at sea

In 1854 the steamer *Olinda* hit Harry Furlough's Rocks and broke up. Fortunately, all those on board were rescued by the Cemlyn Lifeboat.

Another, rather curious wreck occurred at Carmel Head in the early 1740s, when an unknown vessel sank leaving two young boys as the only survivors. They came ashore lashed to a raft, but as they could speak no Welsh or English, they could tell their rescuers nothing about the ship or its crew. One of the boys was adopted by a local family and given the name Evan Thomas. Evan eventually learned to speak Welsh and found that he had a gift for setting bones, which he later developed into a successful business. His descendants founded the Robert Jones and Agnes Hunt Orthopaedic Hospital near Oswestry.

Arctic terns over the Skerries

Nothing is recorded about the second youngster but both boys are assumed to have been Spanish.

Today, the Skerries host a lighthouse perched on the highest point. Now unmanned, it was automated in 1987 and is controlled from Holyhead. The islands are also a popular destination for sea-kayakers and divers who come to explore the many wrecks.

> *"The Skerries is the largest breeding ground of Arctic terns in the country with over 2,000 breeding pairs."*
>
> *BBC Wales*

But the isolated islands are perhaps best known as a bird sanctuary. Protected as an SSSI and by Birdlife International as an 'Important Bird Area', the rocks support large numbers of breeding common, Arctic and roseate terns, as well as gulls, kittiwakes and burrowing puffins. The islands are wardened by the RSPB during the tern breeding season.

Throughout the summer months, rib-ride boats leave Holyhead Marina for trips to North Stack, South Stack and the Skerries.

More information: To visit (but not land on) the Skerries to experience the tern colonies, take a summer RIB ride from Holyhead Marina. Tel: **0333 1234 303**

Rock architecture: *The remarkable rock scenery around the cove at Ynys y Fydlyn*

farmhouse, along the access road, to the lane. Turn right along the lane and in just under ½ mile/1 kilometre turn right onto a track where there is a small parking area. The right of way takes a more or less direct line across large open fields crossing a number of farm tracks to eventually join a track beside conifer woods on the right. Follow this down to the beautiful little cove at Ynys y Fydlyn where you rejoin the coast path.

To continue on the **coastal route**, keep ahead beyond the chimney and mine building over open ground following low marker posts, until the distant Holyhead Mountain comes into view across the bay and you are forced to rise leftwards to a **small rocky summit** above the headland of **Trwyn Cerrigyreryr**.

From here there is a wide view of Holyhead Bay. To the south-west you will see the Irish ferries arriving and leaving Holyhead Harbour as they have done for centuries. Today however, this once hazardous and major undertaking can be completed quite safely in under two hours. Behind the town, Holyhead Mountain rises to 220 metres, the highest point on the island. Further south the chimney at the aluminium works forms a prominent and well known landmark. On clear days, or just before sunset, you can often see the hills of southern Ireland on the western horizon. To the south, the coast becomes less dramatic beyond Church Bay, although the coves between Carmel Head and Porth y Bribys present some of the grandest cliff scenery on the island.

9 Beyond Trwyn Cerrigyreryr, the path continues over open grazing land above the rocky cove of **Porth yr Hwch** before entering a restricted section of path.

Wildfowers

For much of its 870 miles, the Wales Coast Path is like a linear nature reserve. Clifftop paths, salt marshes, dunes and shorelines are often alive with wildflowers throughout the year. Watch for primroses, bluebells and squill in early spring. Summer brings ox-eye daisies, sea pinks, horned poppies, sea holly and wild thyme. And even in autumn, bright berries, ferns and seedheads decorate the path. It's a natural delight.

Remote cove: *The hidden cove at Ynys y Fydlin*

Note: access to the following section is only available between 1 February and 14 September. During closed periods see the detour from Carmel Head on page 115.

The path continues along steep, grassy slopes and then an area of heather and stunted pines to pass a tall concrete post near to the edge of high cliffs overlooking **Ynys y Fydlyn** (the small rocky island to your right). Take care on this section especially in wet or windy weather. Descend to the shingle beach that backs the cove.

This little cove with its shingle beach, crystal clear water and fine rock scenery is an attractive spot. The remoteness of the cove probably means that you will have it to yourself, although you may be watched from the woods by thousands of young pheasants specially bread for the winter shoot. At low tide it is easy enough to get onto Ynys y Fydlyn, from where you will be able to enjoy a fine view of the dramatic rock scenery which surrounds the cove.

The 'Hudiksvall', a Swedish barque foundered on Ynys y Fydlyn in 1890 and the crew of 116 were forced to lash themselves to the upper rails until the Holyhead Lifeboat came to their aid. All lives were saved.

10 At the far end of the cove, the pitched coastal path heads diagonally-right up onto the cliff tops. Continue along a section of open rough grazing land to the next rocky inlet—**Porth y Bribys**. Go through a kissing gate and rise to meet a farm track. Turn right along the track and cross a **small stone bridge**. The farm track bends left immediately after the bridge, but the coast path heads half-right. Follow the most obvious footpath along the coastal slope with broad views out over Holyhead Bay.

The open grazing land ends at a kissing gate close to the cliff edge and the path continues beside fields on the edge of the grassy coastal slope.

11 Cross a footbridge and go through a kissing gate to enter **National Trust land** at **Clegir Mawr**. The path keeps to the outside edge of fields on the left. After steps, the final section before **Church Bay** is cut across steep slopes through scrub. A kissing gate leads into fields above Church Bay. Follow the path along field edges and along an **enclosed footpath** that immediately backs the bay. At the lane turn left.

(For the bus stop in **Llanfaethlu** continue on the coastal path to Porth Trwyn [2 kilometres/1¼ miles]. From Porth Trwyn turn left along the lane, and then right up a public path past 'Plas Y Gwynt'. Go over the stile to the right of the house and bear left up two fields. Go over the ladder stile through an area of woodland, to come out onto a track. Turn right, and right again following the drive to 'Carreglwyd' up to the road into Llanfaethlu. The bus stops on the main road and by the village shop.)

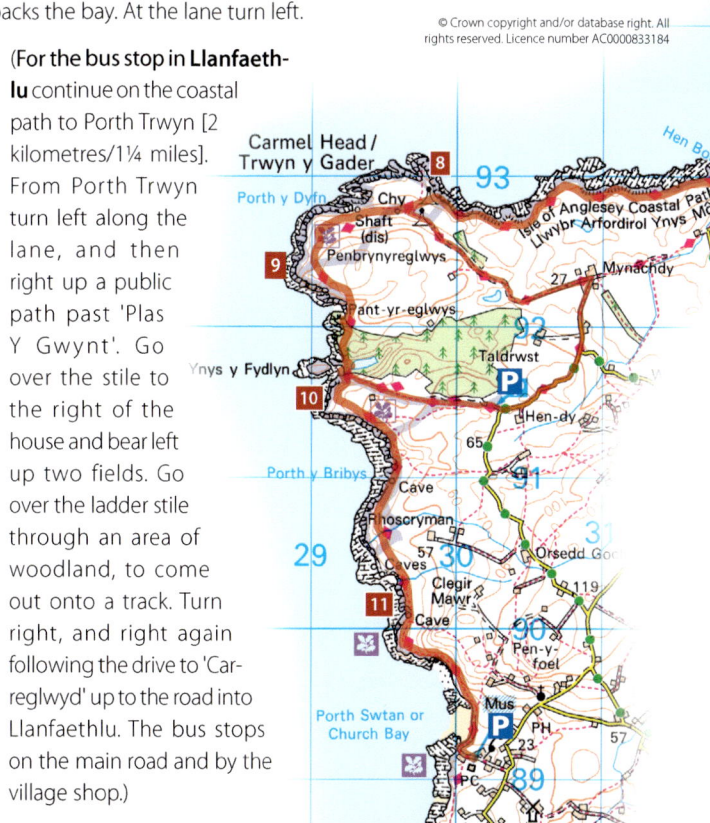

SECTION SEVEN

Church Bay to Holyhead

Distance: *14 miles / 22 kilometres* | **Start:** *Church Bay SH 301 892*
Finish: *Saint Cybi's Church, Holyhead SH 247 826* | **Maps:** *Ordnance Survey Explorer 262 Landranger 114*

Outline: Along but undemanding section along a series of small coves and bays in the approach to Holyhead

This section is fairly flat with several sandy beaches and the coastal path moves into farmland behind the shoreline in a number of places. The walk up the banks of Afon Alaw to the new footbridge is sheltered and rich in birdlife. Beyond the estuary, there is a long stretch over the Stanley Embankment before joining a sheltered path around small cliffs and through the woods of the Penrhos Coastal Park. The remaining mile or two is urban walking into Holyhead.

Services: *Small seasonal shop at Church Bay, but little else en-route. Seasonal café at Penrhos Coastal Park. All services at Holyhead along with public transport links back to Llanfaethlu*

Don't miss: Afon Alaw – small but pretty tidal river on the west coast | Penrhos Coastal Park – wooded country park close to Beddmanarch Bay | **Saint Cybi's Church** – Grade I Listed medieval church within the walls of a Roman fort

▲ *Looking backalong the coast towards Church Bay from Porth Trwyn*

Church Bay

Church Bay is also known as Porth Swtan, thought to mean 'bay of the Whiting', indicating that perhaps large numbers of the fish were landed here at one time. Its English name is most likely to have come from the off-shore view of sailors visiting the nearby port of Holyhead, when it is backed by the prominent spire of the church of Saint Rhyddlad. Today the bay is frequented by summer bathers despite the fact that the upper part of the beach consists mainly of shingle.

Porth Tywyn-mawr one of the many sandy bays on this section of coast

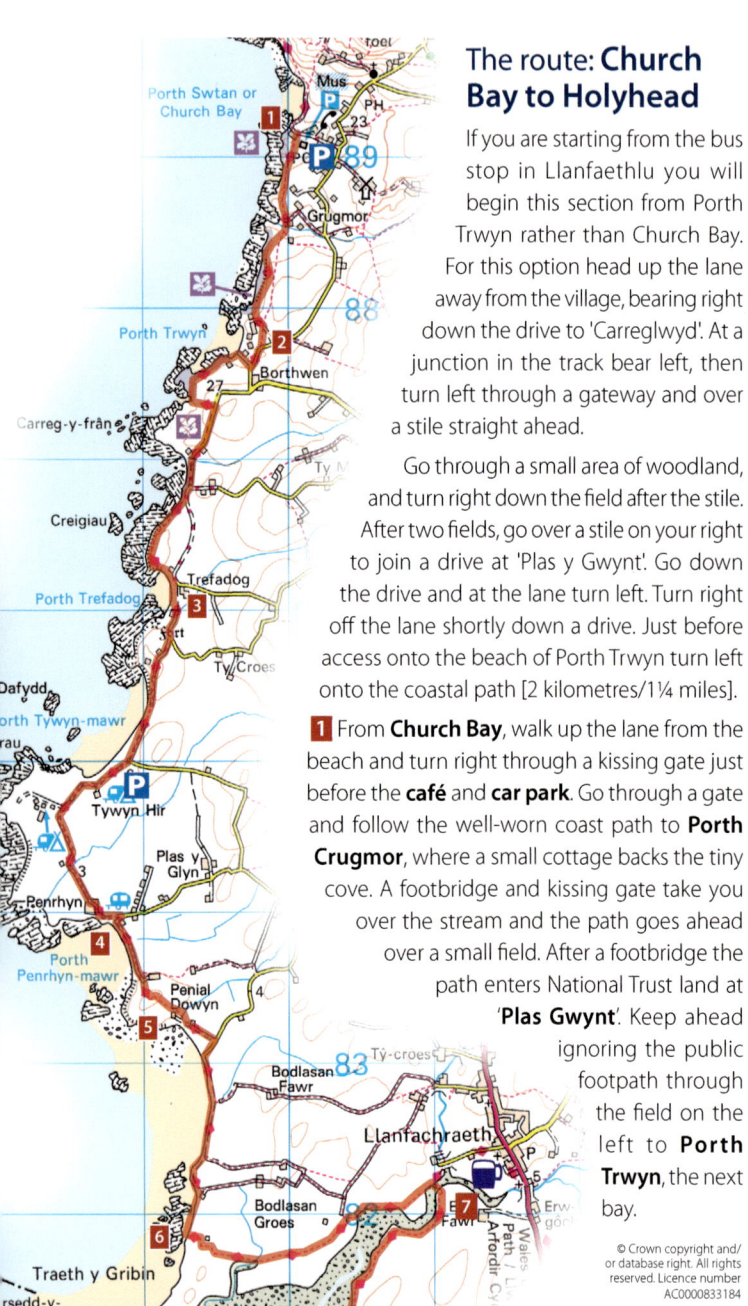

The route: **Church Bay to Holyhead**

If you are starting from the bus stop in Llanfaethlu you will begin this section from Porth Trwyn rather than Church Bay. For this option head up the lane away from the village, bearing right down the drive to 'Carreglwyd'. At a junction in the track bear left, then turn left through a gateway and over a stile straight ahead.

Go through a small area of woodland, and turn right down the field after the stile. After two fields, go over a stile on your right to join a drive at 'Plas y Gwynt'. Go down the drive and at the lane turn left. Turn right off the lane shortly down a drive. Just before access onto the beach of Porth Trwyn turn left onto the coastal path [2 kilometres/1¼ miles].

1 From **Church Bay**, walk up the lane from the beach and turn right through a kissing gate just before the **café** and **car park**. Go through a gate and follow the well-worn coast path to **Porth Crugmor**, where a small cottage backs the tiny cove. A footbridge and kissing gate take you over the stream and the path goes ahead over a small field. After a footbridge the path enters National Trust land at '**Plas Gwynt**'. Keep ahead ignoring the public footpath through the field on the left to **Porth Trwyn**, the next bay.

© Crown copyright and/or database right. All rights reserved. Licence number AC0000833184

Beach diversion: *Two walkers take a break from the coast path and walk one of the many beaches*

Just before houses on the cliffs, turn left through a kissing gate and cut across a small field to the far corner. Go through a kissing gate crossing an access track and head down a path opposite through gorse to a reach lane. Follow the lane ahead to **Porth Trwyn** (about 150 metres).

2 Turn right as signed for the coastal path down an access track and bear left just before the beach (Porth Trwyn). Go through a kissing gate into the **'Trwyn Gwter Fudr'** National Trust land. *This is an open grass headland with wide views across to Holyhead and back along the coast to Carmel Head and The Skerries.*

After a **footbridge** the coast path turns left away from the coast on a fenced path to reach a lane. Turn right along the lane and follow it down past houses at the head of a shingle bay. Where the lane swings left, keep ahead along a farm track. Just before fields, go through a gate on the right onto a fenced path above a shingle beach. This leads around a small headland. At the next bay descend the steps onto the beach at **Porth Trefadog**.

3 Walk down onto the sand and bear left along the beach. At the far end of the bay turn left immediately before a house at the beach access. Walk up the lane and at a fork bear right. Where the lane swings right into a driveway, continue straight ahead along a grassy track which takes you to **Porth Tywyn-mawr** or 'Sandy Beach'.

Walk along the sandy path that backs the bay and at the access road turn right. Head towards the **caravan and camping site**. Go through a kissing gate by the entrance gates and walk ahead on the **site road**. Keep right at a fork and at a T-junction turn right, then immediately left at the beach access. Follow the access road which soon becomes a path between caravan fields. Pass the **tennis courts** and continue ahead along the road passing out of the site by the barriers. Follow the road, passing through **Penrhyn farm**, down to the bay at **Porth Penrhyn-mawr**.

4 The access road bends left by the shingle beach and then heads inland. Bear right off the road here across grass and drop down onto the beach briefly (in front of a **bungalow**) before rising up steps on the left. Go through a gate to join an unsurfaced track and follow this track along the back of the bay. Join a tarmac access road and head towards a **farm**.

Do not follow the road left into the farm, instead, go through a kissing gate straight ahead and walk directly up the following field. Go through the next kissing gate and keep left in the next field to walk down towards a farm—**Peniel Dowyn**—on the edge of the next bay.

Despite a modest height of just 21 metres, there is a fine view of the surrounding countryside from this little hill. To your right, across the wide sweep of Holyhead Bay, the Irish ferries can be seen entering and leaving Holyhead harbour whilst the chimney of the aluminium works provides one of the most visible landmarks on this side of the island. Directly ahead, the distant peaks of Yr Eifl can be seen on the horizon with the higher summits of Snowdonia further to the left.

5 Keep to the left of the farmhouse crossing a stone wall, then bear half-right to a kissing gate in the fence onto the drive. Turn left along the drive. At the end of the drive turn right at a T-junction and walk down onto the beach. Turn left and walk along the sand for almost 1.6 kilometres/1 mile.

6 After passing a slate-clad house almost on the sand—'**Bodardraeth**'—look for a gate on the left (about 350 metres past the house). This leads onto a track which heads towards a **ruined farm building**. About 45 metres along the track turn right through a kissing gate, then bear left along the edge of fields passing to the right of the ruin. The right of way cuts left through an area of heather-covered sand dunes to a kissing gate leading onto an embankment used to prevent flooding of the fields to the left.

The name of nearby Llanfachraeth, which means 'church on or near the little beach or inlet' undoubtedly refers to the small tidal estuary of Afon Alaw. The estuary is 'little' when compared to the large area of tidal sands which stretch between mainland Anglesey and Holy Island.

Go through a kissing gate at the far end of the sea wall and bear half-left through the field to eventually reach a kissing gate on the left. Through the gate, cut directly across the next field to join an access track. Follow the track ahead and in about 150 metres turn right through a kissing gate and walk along the field edge to a kissing gate in the lower right-hand corner. This leads onto the tidal marshes beside **Afon Alaw**. (This may be covered during high tides. If so, return across the field to the access track and turn right along the lane. Follow this lane to Llanfachraeth.)

The path along the marsh edge stays close to the hedge and fence on your left. Further on, a kissing gate leads into a small field—cross the field to a second kissing gate that takes you back onto the marsh edge again. Walk ahead over a raised boardwalk to reach the **footbridge over Afon Alaw**.

7 Cross the footbridge and follow the path right along the southern shore of the Alaw estuary.

At high tide the estuary looks like a large inland lake but at low tide there is very little water at all. The marshes are a good place for bird watching.

There are sections of boardwalk and footbridges along this stretch of path. At a small **muddy inlet** cross a **stone footbridge**, originally built to protect the fields on the left from flooding at high tide.

The Afon Alaw estuary

Arch angel: *Old masonry on the Penrhos Coastal Park with distant view of Holyhead Harbour*

Continue on the path ahead until, just before **Penrhyn Bach Farm**, the path turns right crossing a footbridge to reach an enclosed path on the left that leads beside the farm to reach **Gorad Beach**. Head left along the beach.

8 At the far end of Gorad Beach take the signed coastal path up steps. An enclosed footpath now leads beside gardens to reach the road. Turn left along the road and right at the T-junction. At the top of the hill turn right into **Newlands Park** estate. Keep on the main thoroughfare and as the road curves around to the right into a cul-de-sac go straight ahead along a path between two houses into fields. Cross the fields keeping to the right-hand edge and go through a kissing gate. Descend a set of steps and walk round buildings to emerge on the **A5** at the Stanley Embankment.

Alternative route: *Along the shore*
It is straightforward to continue along the rocky shore from the Gorad Beach to reach the 👁 **Stanley Embankment**, rather than following the signed coastal path inland. This is possible apart from up to two hours either side of high tide.

9 Turn right and cross the **Stanley Embankment**. At the far end, bear right past the **old tollhouse**, which has now been converted into tearooms, and walk through the car park to the **Penrhos Coastal Park**.

The Penrhos Estate was once the seat of the Stanleys, a family that was to have much influence on the development of Holy Island. The Estate was acquired in 1763 following the marriage of Margaret Owen and Sir John Thomas Stanley of Alderley. The land was bought by Anglesey Aluminium Ltd. in 1972 and the area—now known as Penrhos Coastal Park—made accessible to the general public.

Continue along the tarmac footpath beyond the car park and turn left as signed by the **memorial**. Where the path forks, turn right through the gate and follow the path through the woods. Turn right again at the next T-junction (next to a **pet's graveyard**) soon returning to the coast edge.

Soon the path swings away from the coast again and forks. Bear right here to walk to the end of the headland (**Gorsedd-y-penrhyn**) for a view of the bay (continue straight ahead if you want to miss this out).

From the stone seat and wind shelter at the end of the headland you can enjoy wide views taking in much of Holyhead Bay from the distant Skerries away to the north, to ships arriving and leaving Holyhead harbour over to the west.

From the **stone seat and wind shelter** at the end of the headland, continue along the grassy coastal edge, soon entering the trees again to reach a junction with a gravel footpath. Turn right here and soon you reach the access to the attractive **sandy cove** you will have noticed from the headland on the right. The fenced garden and house ahead here is known as the

Shelter from the storm: *The Holyhead lifeboat, cruisers and yachts mingle in Holyhead harbour*

'**Bathing House**'. Bear left past the entrance gates and in about 30 metres, turn right along an enclosed footpath that takes you back onto the coastal edge overlooking **Holyhead Bay**.

10 Follow the coastal path passing various crumbling stone structures including '**The Battery**', a semi-circular stone structure which is possibly a folly associated with the **Penrhos Estate**.

Join the grassy embankment by the **Penrhos Beach car park** opposite the **Aluminium Works**, whose tall chimney has been visible since you left Carmel Head. Turn right along the tarmac footpath behind the embankment.

At the end of the embankment pass a small car park and then bear right past a disused toilet block. The path soon widens out into **playing fields**. Keep to the edge of the playing fields passing a **stone arch** on the right, with a housing estate over to the left. In the far corner of the field, the coast path runs beside a factory on the left. Stay beside the fence on the left ignoring paths on the right. Pass a nursery and keep beside a low wall to reach '**Turkeyshore Road**'. Turn left and follow the road to the **roundabout** at the **ferry terminal**.

11 Cross the ferry access lanes and turn right beside the **red brick railway station** wall. Turn left through the station, signed for the 'Town Centre', and cross the **walkway** over the harbour. Cross the elaborate metal '**Celtic Gateway**' bridge to come out onto **Market Street** in the centre of **Holyhead**. Turn right up the pedestrianised street to arrive at **Saint Cybi's church** where this section ends.

Saint Cybi's Church

Saint Cybi was a cousin of Saint David and founded the church here within the walls of the old Roman Fort in 540 AD. The old fort was probably a wise choice, the site was exposed to Irish invaders and was sacked 400 years later by Vikings and again in 1405 by Henry IV, in an attempt to put down the rebellion of Owain Glyndŵr. The current church was built between the 13th and 16th centuries.

Section Eight

Holyhead to Trearddur

Distance: *11½ miles / 18 kilometres* | **Start:** *Saint Cybi's Church, Holyhead SH 247 826* | **Finish:** *Trearddur SH 255 790* | **Maps:** *Ordnance Survey Explorer 262, Landranger 114*

Outline: A dramatic section of rocky coast with the path passing close to Anglesey's highest point

This is one of the most dramatic sections of the entire coastal path with the greatest height gain—up to 600m/2,000ft if you take in Holyhead Mountain. It is also a section of great contrast; from the busy port of Holyhead, to the isolated expanse of heather-clad cliffs around Holyhead Mountain and beyond.

The path begins in the centre of Holyhead, but the hustle and bustle is soon left behind as you pass through the dramatic cliff scenery of Gogarth Bay towards Holyhead Mountain and the famous lighthouse at South Stack. The huge cliffs which dominate the scenery gradually lose height as you head south slowly giving way to sandy coves on the approach to Trearddur. All-in-all this is a rugged and wildly beautiful section of coast.

Services: *Holyhead is a large town with a variety of shops and supermarkets. Banks, pharmacy, cash machines, cafés, pub and restaurants. Accommodation includes B&B*

Don't miss: **Holyhead Mountain** – highest point on Anglesey with wide views across the island to the mainland | **South Stack Lighthouse** – Iconic lighthouse on a rocky sea stack | **The Range** – ecologically important lowland coastal heath

▲ *Sailing boats moored on the beach in Holyhead harbour*

Holyhead

Holyhead dates back to Roman times, when there is believed to have been a port here guarded by the small coastal fort built in the fourth century; its walls still enclose Saint Cybi's Church. The fort was used in conjunction with the lookout tower on Holyhead Mountain to guard what even then must have been a busy harbour. The late date seems to suggest that it was designed as a defence against the Irish, who began making raids on Wales in the final years of the Roman occupation.

The present port began with the need for a reliable ferry to Ireland to carry the London to Dublin post packets. The big advantage of Holyhead was the short sea crossing—almost half that from the nearest English port. However, poor roads through North Wales tended to minimise this advantage and other ports also ran Irish ferries.

Things improved for Holyhead when Thomas Telford built what is now the A5 and constructed bridges across Afon Conwy and the Menai Strait. With these improvements came the age of rapid travel. Coaches brought travellers in increasing numbers, as well as the Dublin post which could then travel from London to Holyhead in just 48 hours. To cater for all this growth, Parliament passed a Bill enabling a new harbour to be built. By the mid 1800s Stevenson's tubular steel bridge brought the railways to Holyhead with a level of comfort and speed previously unthinkable. The railway station and inner harbour were officially opened by the Prince of Wales in 1880.

Today, Holyhead remains one of the prime ports for Ireland and recent improvements in ferry design has cut the crossing time to just 90 minutes.

An Irish ferry heading for Holyhead

On top of the world: *Two walkers watch a ferry heading for Holyhead from Holyhead Mountain*

The route: Holyhead to Trearddur

1 Leave **Saint Cybi's Church** heading north (with the harbour over to the right) through a gateway in the wall and pass through the car park. At a T-junction turn right ('**Boston Street**') and walk down to the main road. Turn left here and follow the road bearing left with it into '**Prince of Wales Road**' to walk along the **waterfront**. Pass the public toilets on the corner of '**Newry Street**' and head right down towards the **Maritime Museum**.

2 Follow the **Promenade** until you reach the **Lifeboat Station**, then bear left up to the main road again. Turn right, (ignore the road ahead signed to the **Breakwater Country Park**) and follow the lane to its end beside the castellated **Soldier's Point Hotel**. *The building was gutted by fire in September 2011.*

At the end of the road go through a **stone gateway**, turn left and in 100 metres or so, at the end of the building on the left, take the signed coastal path on the right. This leads down to a little cove behind the massive **Breakwater**.

This massive structure, over a mile long, was officially opened by the Prince of Wales in 1873 having taken 28 years to build. It was built as part of an initiative by Parliament to create harbours of refuge all over Britain where passing ships could ride out storms. The stone for its construction was quarried at what is now the Breakwater Country Park.

Section 8: **Holyhead to Trearddur** 135

3 Bear left behind the beach, up steps and through a kissing gate. In a few metres turn right at a junction on the signed path that makes its way around the open headland. Follow the well-defined coastal path now towards Holyhead Mountain ahead.

4 As you approach the quarries on **Holyhead Mountain**, the path swings left to a gate. Go through the gate and keep ahead to reach a broad track. Turn right along the track and almost immediately bear right through a kissing gate beside a large field gate. The path goes ahead through rough grass towards the large **quarry face** ahead.

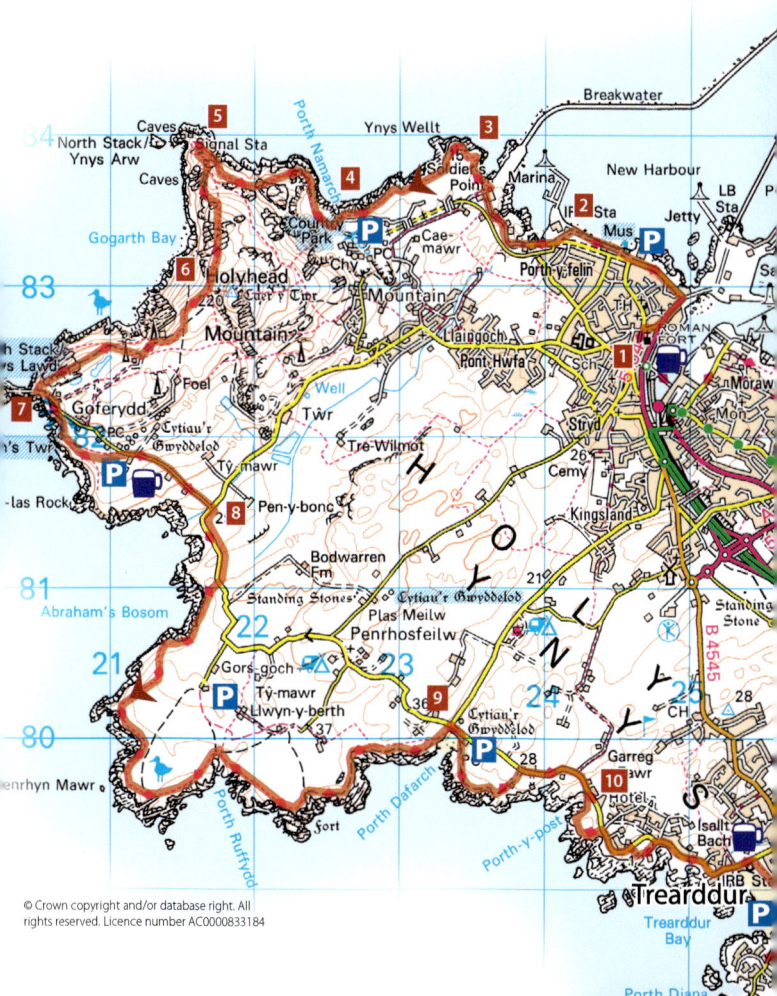

© Crown copyright and/or database right. All rights reserved. Licence number AC0000833184

As you approach the cliff face, the path curves right to a point overlooking the sea with a wide view back to Holyhead harbour. The path swings left here up **stone steps** to contour the open hillside high above the sea. Stay on the pitched path ignoring minor paths here and there and soon you will be able to see along the coast to the buildings at **North Stack**. After the little **magazine building** the path begins a steady rise to a T-junction. Turn right and follow the path towards North Stack. Where the path forks, bear right down to the building at North Stack. (Alternatively, to avoid the descent to visit North Stack, keep ahead. Cross the broad track leading down to North Stack and in a few metres meet the coast path. Turn left.)

Anyone with a head for heights can walk alongside the boundary wall to the end of the rocks for an impressive view of the cliff scenery. Take care near the cliff edge. Looking back you will see the huge cavern that will eventually separate the rock you are now standing on from the main cliff to create another sea stack (similar to South Stack). To the right there is a view along Gogarth Bay where a number of high-grade rock climbs have been recorded and climbers can often be seen dotting the face.

Looking down on South Stack lighthouse

Section 8: **Holyhead to Trearddur** 137

Rugged coast: *This section of coast has some of the highest cliffs in North Wales*

5 From North Stack, walk back to the building and turn right up the track. Where it begins to level the coast path bears right off the track and begins the steady climb, in a series of steps, up towards **Holyhead Mountain**. Ignore minor paths on the right as you rise—these are mainly used by rock climbers to reach the cliffs below.

The path levels as you pass through a **stone wall** then makes a slight drop to a broad saddle. Take the right fork here rising again up onto the shoulder of the mountain.

Detour: *To include the summit of Holyhead Mountain*
At the top of the rise a signed path on the left will take you onto Holyhead Mountain. At the summit the path passes through a jumble of rocks marking the edge of the Iron Age hillfort.

Holyhead Mountain is the highest point on both Holy Island and Anglesey and the view in clear conditions is the most extensive on the island. To the south and east almost the whole of Anglesey can be seen against a backdrop of Snowdonia's highest peaks. A handful of low hills are the only break in the flat contours of the island. South the indented west coast presents a more interesting foreground to the shapely hills of Llŷn.

The base of a Roman watchtower can be seen beside the triangulation

Dramatic coast: *South Stack is famous for its huge sea cliffs and iconic lighthouse*

pillar which is thought to have been used in conjunction with the small coastal fort in Holyhead. Also to be seen around the summit are the remains of an Iron Age hillfort. Both the fort and the tower date from the fourth century, a period when the coast of Wales came under increasing attack from Irish invaders. As an early warning against such attacks from the west, this elevated viewpoint is unrivalled; in very clear conditions the Wicklow Mountains can be seen on the far horizon.

To return to the coastal path, retrace your steps back down to the broad traversing path and turn left towards South Stack.

6 The path continues ahead, soon much broader with a good gravel surface. Ignore paths on either side and after passing a **fenced modern stone building** up to the right, cross the access road. Follow the stony footpath opposite passing close to brick buildings on the left beneath a radio mast.

This path drops slightly then rises to pass along a rounded heather ridge with a small pool down to the left. Soon you will find yourself in a dramatic position overlooking **South Stack Lighthouse** from beside the ruins of the **old telegraph station**. Head half-left from here to reach a road end directly above the lighthouse.

7 Turn left along the road and at the next car park bear right down to **Ellin's Tower**.

The tower was built as a summer retreat for Ellin, the wife of William Stanley in 1867. Ellin was a keen observer of the bird life to be found around South Stack and her husband, who was the liberal MP for Anglesey from 1837-74, was responsible for several archaeological excavations on Holyhead Mountain. Dur-

'Irishmen's huts'?

Opposite the RSPB car park entrance, a gate leads into a small field where several prehistoric hut circles can be seen. Known as 'Cytiau 'r Gwyddelod' or the 'Irishmen's Huts' they may date from a short period of colonisation by Irish sea raiders following the Roman withdrawal. It was on Anglesey that these raiders were finally defeated and expelled by Cadwallon in AD 470.

ing their lifetime, the couple also provided Holyhead with a hospital, a home for sailors, the Market Hall and the town's water supply. Ellin died in 1876 and her husband eight years later.

Ellin's Tower became a popular attraction in the closing years of the nineteenth and early twentieth centuries, before falling into decay after World War II. It was later bought by the RSPB, renovated and opened as an information centre and bird hide in 1982.

Birds that can be seen here in large numbers include guillemots, which favour the crowded, narrow ledges, and puffins, often found on the steep grassy slopes above the cliffs. Other regular visitors include fulmars, razorbills, shags, Manx shearwaters and herring gulls.

Pass **Ellin's Tower**, and join the cliff path taking care near the cliff edges. At a junction of paths, turn left up to the **RSPB car park**. Pass through the car park, and turn right along the lane.

8 At the T-junction go straight across the road, through a little gate opposite and up the bank on the signed coast path. Bear right and follow the fenced footpath parallel with the lane.

At the end of the path cross the lane and go through a kissing gate opposite into fields. Bear left keeping to the edge of the fields—the cliffs out of sight behind the earth covered wall on the right. At the far end of the fields cross a sleeper bridge and go through another gate into the open heathland at **The Range** (part of South Stack Cliffs Nature Reserve). Follow the broad path ahead.

At the far end of the headland the path swings left and continues close to the cliffs. Take care in poor weather as this section is heavily indented with rocky coves and gorges.

Keep following the coast to eventually go through a kissing gate. More open, grassy cliff tops follow until you reach another kissing gate. Go through the gate, across a small field, then back onto the open cliff top path after another kissing gate near a small rocky cove.

The path continues eventually passing a **caravan park** and along a section of path above the beach at **Porth Dafarch** to reach the road. There are public toilets here and a snack van during the summer.

9 Cross the back of the bay and bear right onto the signed coastal path again. Walk around this smaller headland and as you approach a house, cross a wooden footbridge and kissing gate and walk along an enclosed path to

Section 8: **Holyhead to Trearddur** 141

Distant view: *Looking back to South Stack Lighthouse from The Range*

join the driveway. Turn left up the drive to the road. Turn right along the road following it to the next sandy cove, **Porth y Post**.

10 From here the path continues around another headland on the outside edge of fenced fields to **Porth y Pwll**.

Turn right along the road and as a large house comes into view, bear right along a lane that shortly loops back to rejoin the road. Turn right and follow the road to **Trearddur**. As you approach Trearddur turn right by the **Lifeboat Station** and walk along the **promenade** which immediately backs the beach where this section ends.

Section nine

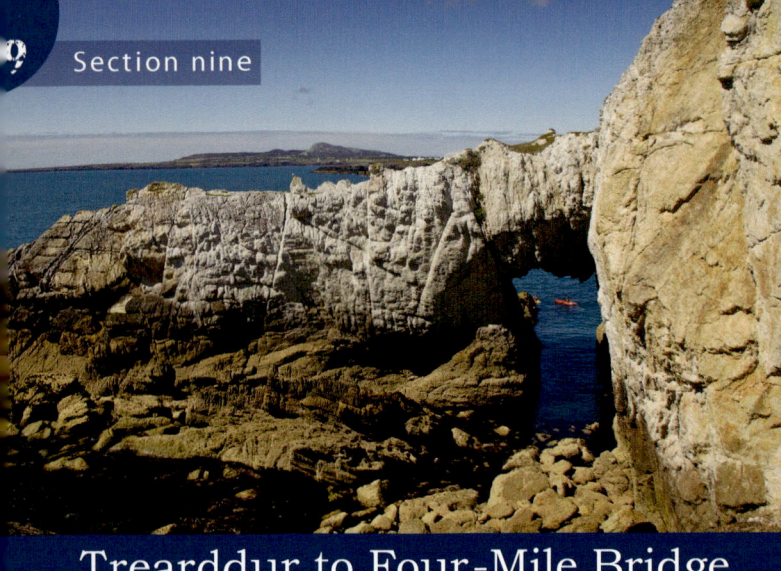

Trearddur to Four-Mile Bridge

Distance: *14 kilometres/8¾ miles* | **Start:** *Trearddur SH 255 790* | **Finish:** *Four-Mile-Bridge SH 280 783* | **Maps:** *Ordnance Survey Explorer 262, Landranger 114*

Outline: A walk of two halves: a series of coves and cliffs between Trearddur and Rhoscolyn, followed by farmland and marshes

The immediate vicinity of Trearddur is highly developed, but you soon leave this behind for a coastline that is rugged, indented and adorned with unusual rock formations and small coves. The cliffs gradually gain height to reach a climax at Rhoscolyn Head with its wide views and nearby sea arch.

The sandy bays of Borthwen at Rhoscolyn and Silver Bay follow, before the path turns inland to Four-Mile Bridge, passing through a mixture of quiet lanes, farmland and salt marsh.

Services: *Very little on the route once you leave Trearddur behind. Excellent dog friendly pub (The White Eagle) at Rhoscolyn serving food each day. Check opening times off season. Very little at Four-Mile Bridge some accommodation, campsite. Bus links back to Holyhead and Valley.*

👁 **Don't miss:** Bwa Du and Bwa Gwyn sea arches – impressive rock arches near Rhoscolyn Head | St Gwenfaen's Well – Medieval healing well

▲ *The impressive Bwa Gwyn sea arch near Rhoscolyn*

Trearddur and Rhoscolyn

Trearddur is one of Anglesey's most popular resorts, particularly for water sports such as sailing and windsurfing. A shallow channel may once have divided Holy Island in two at this point and even now the water of the 'inland sea' between the Stanley Embankment and Four-Mile Bridge can be seen from the road just 400m to the east. Prevailing westerly winds have filled this in and formed the fine beach around which the village has developed.

Like Trearddur, Rhoscolyn is also popular with watersports enthusiasts but, tucked away at the southern tip of Holy Island, is much quieter and lacks the 'resort' atmosphere of Trearddur. The rocky coastline between the two is full of interest, with two notable sea arches—Bwa Gwyn the *white arch*, and Bwa Ddu the *black arch*, reflecting the colour of the composite rock.

The quiet bay at Rhoscolyn

The route: **Trearddur to Four-Mile-Bridge**

1 This section starts with a walk along the promenade which backs the bay in **Trearddur**. At the far end, turn right and walk along '**Ravenspoint Road**'.

Alternative route: *Around the headland to Porth Diana*

There are permissive paths around the small headlands on the right which may be followed instead of the road, but not all lead back to the road. The first one is the best, through a gap in the low wall and down steps, it leads around the headland on the outside of walled gardens, with good views back to the bay and along the rocky coast to Penrhyn Mawr. It meets the road again at **Porth Diana**.

Section 9: **Trearddur to Four-Mile Bridge** 145

Storm light: *Dark skies loom over the long sandy beach at Trearddur Bay*

2 The road eventually ends at open ground with the signs to '**Tŷn Rhôs Camping Site**' and '**Lee Caravan Park**' to the left and right. A footpath sign indicates the right of way which takes a direct line just to the left of the road to Lee Caravan Park. In around 40 metres, turn right, soon beside a **wall** on the right heading off across the **open heather heath** towards the sea. At the end of the wall, swing left on a well-defined path across the open heath.

The official route is marked by the usual yellow topped posts. Soon you are on the open rocky coast again and it comes as a bit of a surprise to see a large **static caravan site** in a hollow below. Bear left with the caravans down to your right and immediately before the site access road, turn right on the signed coast path down between the caravans and cross the access road. Opposite, go through a kissing gate and walk along grassy back of the tiny shingle bay at **Porth-y-garan**.

3 Join a track by two large **stone gateposts** on the left and turn right passing a small reedy pool on your left.

> **Alternative route:** *A short loop keeping closer to the coast*
> Bear right after the gateposts following a short loop joining the main path after the small pool.

At a tiny nameless **cove** on the right, keep right beside the fence and cross

Sea arch: *Sea kayakers paddle through the impressive Bwa Gwyn sea arch*

the cove by two kissing gates. Follow the yellow-topped waymarker posts over open ground now, soon curving inland beside a **stone wall** on your right around a large house. Bear right across the drive and over a stone stile between two sets of **stone gate pillars**. Keep left off the drive beside the boundary wall on the left, then pass through a gap in the far corner. Keep left here through open ground to a kissing gate in the wall. Walk through a grazing field to a wooden kissing gate with a sea arch—**Bwa Du**—partly hidden to your right.

4 The path is obvious and well-walked now taking a direct line through grazing fields past another sea arch— 👁 **Bwa Gwyn**—to the inlet of **Porth Saint**.

Bwa Gwyn is more impressive than Bwa Du. The names: 'white arch' and 'black arch', describe the colour of the rock, so it is immediately obvious which is which.

After a kissing gate and short section of pitching the path keeps close to a well-built **stone wall** on the left with cliffs to the right all the way to Rhoscolyn Head. Take care near a number of deep inlets.

5 Stay beside the wall as it curves left after **Rhoscolyn Head** and take care on the final section before the kissing gate where the gap between the wall and the cliffs on the right becomes much narrower! The path is visible now as it crosses open ground aiming directly for the **Coastguard Lookout** and passing **Saint Gwenfaen's Well** (see inset box below).

The Coastguard Lookout, a little further on, is no longer in use but its position, unsurprisingly, enjoys a magnificent panorama across much of the west coast of Anglesey and Holy Island. The hazardous nature of this coastline can

Holy Well

The small stone enclosure on the clifftop near Rhoscolyn Head is Saint Gwenfaen's Well; the remains of a medieval healing well. It has stone steps, corner seats and may have originally been roofed. During the Middle Ages, like so many other sites, it became a place of pilgrimage—a gift of two white quartz pebbles thrown into the pool were believed to cure mental health problems.

Lookout: *The old Coastguard Lookout near Rhoscolyn Head*

be appreciated from here and at certain points of the tide numerous rocks and reefs are visible.

Pass to the left of the Coastguard Lookout, following the signed coast path directly down sloping grazing fields (distant small square tower ahead). After a kissing gate, cross the access road to '**The Point**' and continue ahead on a wall-enclosed path eventually between gardens, and finally turning right across a lawn to reach the road by stone gate posts at '**Bryn Eithin**'.

6 Follow the access road between houses and past a tiny cove on the right to reach **Borthwen**—the main beach at **Rhoscolyn**. Borthwen can be walked most of the time but if the water is too high, look for steps on the left in a few metres that lead up to a path along the top of a retaining sea wall, rejoining the beach by the entrance to the car park.

Turn left through the **car park** (public toilets) and continue along the lane. *(To visit 'The White Eagle' pub, continue up the lane. Return to this point to continue.)*

At the first bend turn right onto the signed coast path and follow the path along the back of the bay. At a fork, keep ahead (right) and follow the path to join a track leading to houses on the right ('**Cil Bwch**'). Walk left along the track and at a T-junction turn right. Pass between the houses and almost at the end of the track (beside '**Borth Esgob**') go through the kissing gate ahead onto the **open coastal heath**. Follow the well-defined path ahead marked by yellow-topped posts.

Dropping down into the tiny shingle cove of **Porth Gorslwyn**, go over three small sleeper bridges, head up through gorse and cross a field to a kissing gate. Follow the well-defined path around another headland of coastal heath all the way to **Silver Bay**.

7 Turn right down the access ramp onto the beach. Bear left along the sand and in about 250 metres, turn left up **timber steps** into a **small pine wood**. Follow a fenced path through the trees ahead.

Beyond the wood, keep ahead through a kissing gate and along a **wooden boardwalk** to a kissing gate into a field. Go through the gate and head across the field towards the buildings of **Bryn-y-bar**. Pass to the right of the buildings to join the access track. Follow the track ahead.

8 The track becomes a tarmac lane and in about 1 kilometre there is a signed path on the right.

Between 1st October and 31st January you will need to carry straight on along the road turning right at two junctions to reach the other end of an off-road option (below), available during the spring and summer period only.

Spring and summer route: *Avoiding the road section*
To follow the off-road option, turn right off the road here, through a foot gate and follow the path through an area of saplings and scrub. The path is obvious and crosses several **boardwalks** over marshy sections. The path eventually turns left and continues to join the road. Turn right along the road.

9 Follow the road for about 600 metres, before turning right down the access road to '**Rhyd-y-Bont Bach**' farm. Follow the track to the farm.

As you approach the farm, and immediately before the **cattle grid**, bear right onto the signed footpath. This passes beside the garden and exits into a field. Walk ahead through the field keeping to the left of a pond and just before the marshes, turn left through a gate into an area of scrub. Exit into a small field and bear right to pass a **house** almost on the marsh edge. Turn left along a **boardwalk** which keeps close to the edge of the salt marsh. The boardwalk keeps you above wet ground and leads all the way to **Four-Mile Bridge** where this section ends.

10 Section ten

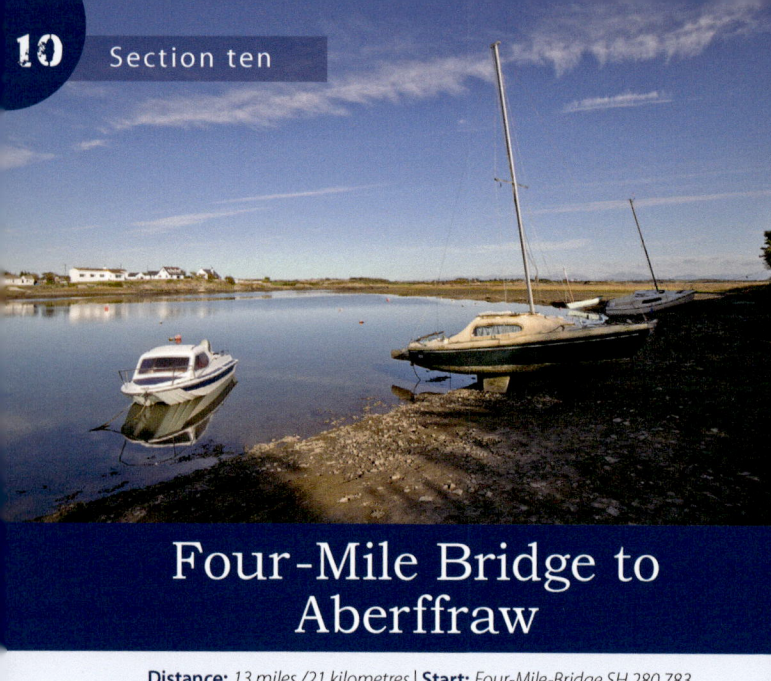

Four-Mile Bridge to Aberffraw

Distance: *13 miles /21 kilometres* | **Start:** *Four-Mile-Bridge SH 280 783*
Finish: *Aberffraw SH 355 689* | **Maps:** *Ordnance Survey Explorer 262, Landranger 114*

Outline: After a mix of farmland and tidal inlets the walk continues with beach walking and a lovely rocky section in the approach to Aberffraw

An unusual start with a section mainly on the level around the tidal estuary separating Holy Island from Anglesey. The aircraft at RAF Valley will announce their presence long before you see the airfield and will accompany you all the way to the well known resort of Rhosneigr, offering a perfect mid-route break.

Beach walking continues beyond Rhosneigr separated by the headland of Mynydd Mawr with its famous Neolithic burial chamber. The path heads inland around the Anglesey Racing Circuit to reach the coast again at Porth Cwyfan with its tiny islanded church. The final section to Aberffraw is rocky and wild with wide views to Snowdonia.

Services: *Rhosneigr provides an idea mid-section break and has pubs, cafés and late shop. Pub, small shop and accommodation at Aberffraw.*

Don't miss: Barclodiad y Gawres – Neolithic burial chamber | Saint Cwyfan's Church – Tiny Celtic church in a wonderful location on a tiny island at Porth Cwyfan

▲ *The tidal estuary at Four-Mile Bridge*

Four-Mile-Bridge

Four-Mile Bridge is also known as Pontrhydbont, or the 'bridge of the ford', indicating the existence of an early crossing between Holy Island and Anglesey. The bridge itself has been in existence for centuries and is shown as one of the alternative routes to Holyhead for those heading for Ireland on the maps of John Ogilby published in 1675. Until the construction of the Stanley Embankment during Thomas Telford's improvement of the London to Holyhead road in the early nineteenth century, this was the only way onto Holy Island without an often dangerous crossing of the tidal sands which separate the two islands.

The construction of the Stanley Embankment has created an 'inland sea' or large tidal lagoon between the two bridges which is often used by canoeists and windsurfers.

Low tide uncovers sandbanks in the Inland Sea.

Quiet waters: *The sheltered, shallow tidal estuary separating Holy Island from Anglesey*

The route: **Four-Mile-Bridge to Aberffraw**

1 Cross the bridge heading towards **Valley** and in about 300 metres or so, look for a farm access road on the right signed for the coastal path (opposite 'Pen-y-Bont' campsite). Walk down the track and bear right through a kissing gate adjacent to the **farm**. The footpath bears left through the field with marshes to the right. As you approach a **small quarry**, keep to the right-hand side where two kissing gates take you across gorse-covered banks and then over a **small stone causeway**. After the causeway, continue straight ahead on a marked footpath through an area of gorse and bracken. The path is well-worn and the line is easy to follow.

A kissing gate takes you into a field—walk straight ahead across the field and down to a kissing gate to join the access road to a house on the left—'**Tyddyn-y-cob**'.

2 Go ahead here through a gate and cross the **dam** with a **pool** to your left. At the end of the dam keep ahead through a field and cross a stone wall in the corner by stone steps. Go ahead in the following field for about 75 metres before turning right over a **stone footbridge** and steps. Follow a wooden walkway over boggy ground and continue straight ahead up the field to enter a quiet lane.

Section 10: **Four-Mile Bridge to Aberffraw**

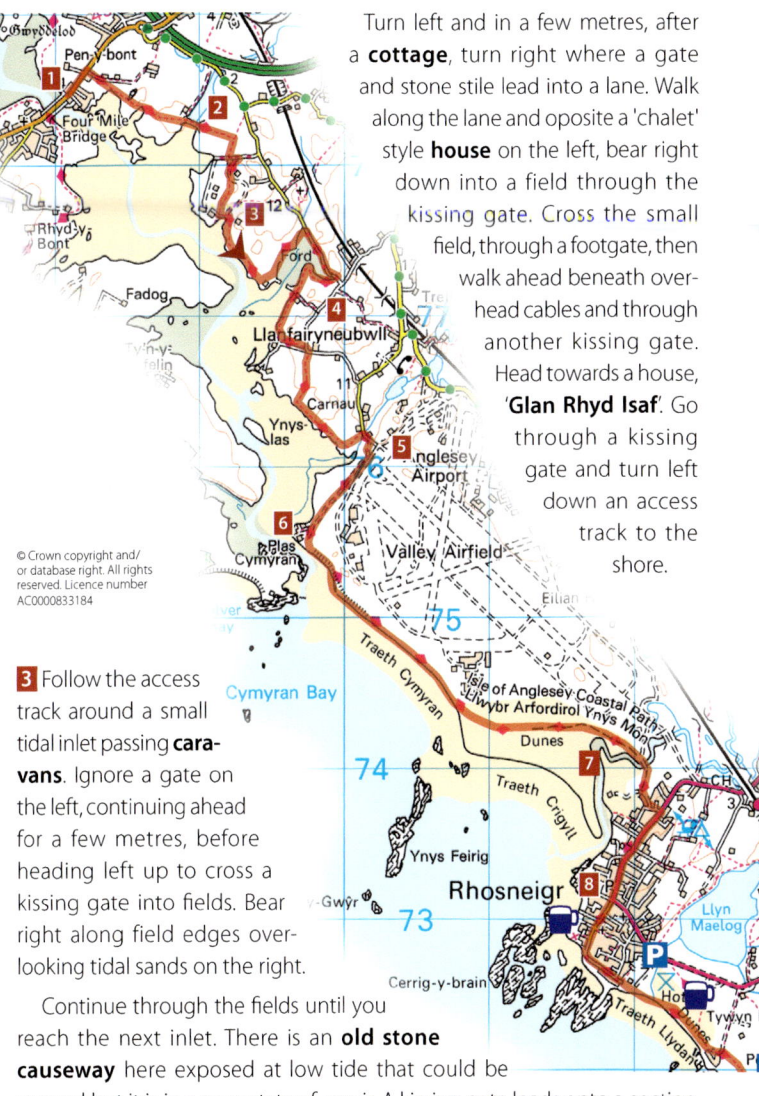

Turn left and in a few metres, after a **cottage**, turn right where a gate and stone stile lead into a lane. Walk along the lane and oposite a 'chalet' style **house** on the left, bear right down into a field through the kissing gate. Cross the small field, through a footgate, then walk ahead beneath overhead cables and through another kissing gate. Head towards a house, '**Glan Rhyd Isaf**'. Go through a kissing gate and turn left down an access track to the shore.

3 Follow the access track around a small tidal inlet passing **caravans**. Ignore a gate on the left, continuing ahead for a few metres, before heading left up to cross a kissing gate into fields. Bear right along field edges overlooking tidal sands on the right.

Continue through the fields until you reach the next inlet. There is an **old stone causeway** here exposed at low tide that could be crossed but it is in a poor state of repair. A kissing gate leads onto a section of fenced path above the shore that leads to an old tidal lane at the head of the creek. (At low tide you can also drop down and walk along the shore to reach the same place.) Go ahead across the lane and bear right onto a path that crosses the head of the creek just above the shore.

Sand dunes: *Approach to Rhosneigr is through the dunes of Traeth Crigyll*

4 At a T-junction with a tarmac lane turn right along the lane and bear right in about 70 metres or so onto the signed coastal path. Up steps, the path is fenced until you reach a kissing gate. Go through the gate and follow the path along the edge of fields with marshes on the right.

At a junction of footpaths near a **cottage** (with the stone causeway seen earlier down to the right), continue ahead along the field edge. As you approach **cottages ahead**, the path swings left away from the estuary up the edge of the field to a kissing gate in the top corner.

Go through the kissing gate into the lane and turn right. In a few metres go through another kissing gate into fields on the right. Walk ahead through the field eventually passing through a gateway. Passing the **landing lights to RAF Valley**, follow the hedge/fence on your left down to a footbridge near the shore. Cross the **footbridge** on the left and keep to the edge of the fields with the tidal sands on your right until you approach the final row of landing lights. Bear left towards the **large house** visible to your left. Go through a kissing gate in front of the house and turn right along the lane.

5 Pass the end of the **airfield runway** and walk down the rough sandy road to the houses at **Cymyran** and on to **Traeth Cymyran**.

Section 10: **Four-Mile Bridge to Aberffraw** 155

6 Turn left and walk along the sand for 3.5 kilometres/1½ miles.

For some time now you will have been aware of your approach to RAF Valley by the numerous low flying fighter planes coming in over the water between here and Holy Island. During the construction of an extension to one of the runways at the air base in 1943, one of the most remarkable Iron Age finds in the country was unearthed. See the box on page 158.

It was on this beach that Rhosneigr's most famous shipwreck occurred in

RAF Valley

The RAF airfield at Valley was built during the Second World War and used to launch European bombing missions and defence sorties. It has continued as an important air base ever since. The RAF's air, sea and mountain rescue service for North Wales is based here and a new facility opened in 2007 to handle public flights (Anglesey Airport/Maes Awyr Môn).

March 1883. The ship in question was the 'Norman Court', a tea-clipper and sister ship to the more famous 'Cutty Sark'. She was built in 1869 and at the time of her final voyage was on the return journey from Java to Greenock on the Firth of the Clyde carrying 1,100 tons of sugar.

On 29 March she was blown off course and became trapped in Cymyran Bay. All attempts to turn the ship around failed and she ran aground at 7pm with such force that half the rigging came down rendering the lifeboats useless. All attempts to launch the Rhosneigr lifeboat failed in the heavy seas and the crew were left clinging to the rigging until the following day. At first light another attempt to launch the lifeboat was made which almost ended in disaster when one of the crew was washed overboard.

By this time the crew of the Holyhead lifeboat had arrived by train and managed to reach the stricken ship in the Rhosneigr lifeboat, rescuing all but two of the crew who had died from exposure during the night. In all, twenty lives were saved.

7 The final approach to **Rhosneigr** is blocked by **Afon Crigyll**, a tidal river that can normally be paddled quite easily. However, the official route avoids this by turning left into the sand dunes where the coast path is signed just after the rocky island of **Ynys Feirig**. Follow the well-walked path, past the boundary fence to **RAF Valley** and head for the **footbridge**.

Cross the footbridge and turn right along a gravel path to reach a road end. Walk along the road and at a T-junction and turn left. At the main road in Rhosneigr turn right and follow the road into the village centre to the crossroads by the **town clock.**

Clear waters at Traeth Cymran

Summer colours: *The superb beach at Rhosneigr and the mouth of Afon Crigyll*

Afon Crigyll has a rather sinister association with an occupation for which this part of Anglesey was particularly notorious in the past—wrecking. During the age of sail this coastline was treacherous enough with many hundreds of ship wrecks recorded. These wrecks were often plundered by locals who are said to have robbed victims and left them to die on the beach. Not satisfied with these occasional 'windfalls' a group know as the 'Crigyll Wreckers' are said to have lured many ships onto the nearby rocks with false beacons and then plundered the wrecks before help could arrive.

Rhosneigr

Rhosneigr has been a popular resort since the closing years of the nineteenth century when a small station on the Holyhead rail line gave visitors access to what would otherwise have been a very remote corner of the island. Prior to this, Rhosneigr was a tiny fishing settlement.

The name Rhosneigr is thought to be derived from 'Yneigr' a maiden's name and 'rhos' meaning moor—its English translation would thus be 'Moor of the Maid'. The word 'Rhos' appears in many Welsh place names and moors are still a familiar part of the Welsh landscape. In Rhosneigr's case the 'moor' referred to is undoubtedly the large area of dunes to the north of the village known as Tywyn Trewan. In earlier centuries this area would have been a wilderness of salt marsh, brackish lakes and sands, occasionally inundated by high tides. Centuries of dune

An Iron Age slave chain found in Llyn Cerrig Bach

Amgueddfa Cymru / National Museum Wales

Sacrificial lake?

Remarkable Iron Age hoard at Llyn Cerrig Bach

During the construction of an extension to one of the runways at the RAF Valley air base in 1943, one of Britain's most remarkable Iron Age finds came to light.

The rare discovery consisted of more than 150 iron, bronze and gold artefacts, including ornaments, tools, weapons and even slave chains. There were parts of a chariot too, as well as large quantities of animal bones. The items are thought to have been deposited into what was then a shallow lake, long before the build up of sand dunes. At first it was thought that these items had been lost in the marshes, but as their numbers grew it became apparent that such a concentration of items within such a small area could only have been placed there intentionally.

The finds date from around the second century BC to the middle of the first century AD and it is now believed that they were placed there as votive offerings, perhaps as part of sacrificial rituals. Anglesey was, after all, the spiritual centre of the Druid religion during this period and the dates of the later finds coincide with the abrupt end of the Druids at the hands of the Roman general Suetonius about AD 61.

More information: *Prehistoric Anglesey: the archaeology of the island to the Roman conquest.* Frances Lynch, 1970

Local beach: *Walking along the shore at Rhosneigr*

formation have since provided a defence from the sea and created an ideal location for the RAF airbase which now occupies the western half of the common.

8 Walk straight ahead on along '**Lôn Traeth Llydan**' (with the **Post Office** and local stores on the right) through the village, then stay with the road as it swings left above the rocky shore. Where the road turns left at the beach access slip, walk ahead down onto the wide sands of **Traeth Llydan**. This beach is walkable at nearly all states of the tide and gives fine views along the coast and across Caernarfon Bay to the hills of the Llŷn Peninsula.

You have the choice of walking either the beach or the dunes here. The beach involves walking along Traeth Llydan and the following two stretches of sand separated by low rocks to join the coastal path around the headland of Mynydd Mawr.

For the dune option, walk ahead along the beach for around 100 metres, and bear left into the dunes where the coast path is signed immediately after the last house on the left. At a sandy track bear right towards picnic benches, cross a **footbridge** just beyond them, and take a direct line straight ahead through the dunes. Head for the large roof you can see ahead. This is **The Oystercatcher pub**. The path passes to the right of the pub heading towards telegraph poles. Pass through a flat grassy area to emerge behind a number of large houses at **Cerrig y Defaid**. Follow the path straight ahead,

160 Wales Coast Path: **ISLE OF ANGLESEY**

Don't miss the opportunity for a mid-walk break at The Oystercatcher, situated in the dunes behind Traeth Lydan

© Crown copyright and/or database right. All rights reserved. Licence number AC0000833184

crossing an access road. Go ahead again through a kissing gate and on over the grassy backs of the dunes to reach the **Tywyn Fferam beach car park** where there is a seasonal beach bar. Walk through the car park and follow a narrow footpath ahead through the dunes to emerge by houses at **Porth Nobla** (the beach option joins here). At a path junction immediately after a small cottage on the left turn right and follow the path around the headland of **Mynydd Mawr**.

Section 10: **Four-Mile Bridge to Aberffraw** 161

Sheltered bay: *Porth Trecastell (Cable Bay)*

At the end of the headland is one of the most famous prehistoric relics on the island—Barclodiad y Gawres. A fine burial chamber from the Neolithic period and in one of the most magnificent settings, it was 'restored' following excavation in the 1950s. A modern entrance and iron gate allow the visitor access to the inner chamber which is covered by a large concrete roof quite out of character with the ancient stones of the original mound. This restoration work has however protected one of the most important features of the chamber—a number of stones decorated with spirals, zig-zags and lozenges. These features link it with the Irish tombs found in the Boyne valley. The name translates into 'Giantess's Apron full' and referred to the large number of stones which were undoubtedly part of the original mound. The chamber is locked but a key is available for a small deposit from The Wayside shop in nearby Llanfaelog.

9 Continue round into **Porth Trecastell** (Cable Bay) to reach the beach car park.

Take the signed coast path on the right at the far end of the car park. This weaves along the coast as far as a point just beyond **Ynysoedd Duon**—the two rocky islets just offshore (about 1 kilometre/¾ mile).

10 Shortly after you have passed the two rocky islets, the path swings left up to a kissing gate. Go through the gate and follow the left-hand field boundary. Turn right in the top corner of the field to a kissing gate by two

Island sanctuary: *Saint Cwyfan's Church on its tiny island*

telegraph poles into a lane. Through the gate, turn right and follow the lane down towards the **Anglesey Motor Racing Circuit**. At the entrance gates, in around 150 metres, turn left onto an unsurfaced lane and follow this down to the secluded bay of **Porth Cwyfan** with its ancient church and tiny walled island cut off at high tide. Bear left along the beach.

11 At the far end of the bay pick up the coastal path again and follow this along a series of low cliffs and flat rocks to the little headland of **Trwyn Du** overlooking the bay at **Aberffraw**.

This is one of the most beautiful bays in Wales and is seen at its best on a clear summer evening when the crowds have gone. Across the shallow clear waters of Caernarfon Bay, the blue outlines of Yr Eifl and the higher peaks of Snowdonia peep over the headland at the end of the bay.

Some of the earliest prehistoric finds on Anglesey have been made here consisting of flint tools and signs of a short occupation by nomadic hunters of the Mesolithic period. With lower sea levels, this is thought to have been an inland site at the time, with an outlook very different to the landscape of today.

12 A kissing gate on the far side of the headland leads onto a footpath that follows the **tidal creek**. Beyond a **cottage** on the shoreline, the path follows the top of an embankment, still parallel to the river.

At the end of the wall, bear left between houses and gardens. Turn right by the entrance to 'Y Cei' and then left along the lane by the river's edge to the **old bridge** on the at Aberffraw where this section finishes.

St Cwyfan's Church

Staint Cwyfan's is a tiny Celtic church in a remarkable setting. Founded in the seventh century it was rebuilt in stone during the twelfth century and fully restored in the nineteenth century. Despite this, it has managed to retain its original simple form. The stone wall which surrounds the island was built during the nineteenth century restoration to counteract severe erosion problems.

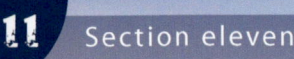

Section eleven

Aberffraw to Newborough

Distance: *19.5 kilometres / 12 miles* | **Start:** *Aberffraw SH 355 689*
Finish: *Llyn Rhos-ddu SH 426 640* | **Maps:** *Ordnance Survey Explorer 262 & 263, Landranger 114*

Outline: A beautiful and spectacular section along two of the finest beaches on the island: Aberffraw and Newborough

This section starts with either a quiet lane through the sand dunes or a walk along the beach at Aberffraw. The next section of coast is occupied by the Bodorgan Estate so the path turns inland along lanes to the village of Malltraeth. A pub and café here make an ideal break before the plantations of the Newborough Forest and the Newborough National Nature Reserve bring a complete contrast. A stunning beach walk along with the option to leave the woods and visit the island of Ynys Llanddwyn make this one of the finest sections of the coast path. Again, the mountains of Snowdonia and the hills of the Llŷn Peninsula lend a powerful and stunning backdrop to the walking.

Services: *There is a pub, café and fish & chip shop at Malltraeth. Pub, late shop at Newborough. B&B accommodation and camping at Newborough*

👁 **Don't miss: Traeth Mawr** – large stunning beach at Aberffraw | **Newborough Forest** – Vast coastal pine forest and nature reserve | **Ynys Llanddwyn & Newborough Beach** – Stunning island and beach with magnificent views to Snowdonia and Llŷn

▲ *Traeth Mawr, one of Anglesey's finest beaches*

Aberffraw

You will find nothing at Aberffraw today to suggest its past importance as the administrative centre for the kings and princes of Gwynedd. Yet for 800 years, Welsh kings and princes used the royal palace here as a base in their fight against invasions from Irish, Saxons, Vikings and finally Normans.

Aberffraw even enjoyed a brief period of prosperity as a small port. Over the centuries, however, the estuary has become filled with wind-blown sand creating one of the largest dune systems on the island and arguably its finest beach at Traeth Mawr. On a fine summer evening the view across the bay to the hills of Llŷn is one of Anglesey's most memorable sights.

Traeth Mawr and the hills of Llŷn

Beautiful beach: *A view of Traeth Llanddwyn framed by pine woods*

The route: **Aberffraw to Llyn Rhos-ddu**

1 Cross the little stone bridge to the car park by the common.

Alternative route: *A detour along Aberffraw's superb beach*
At most states of the tide you can follow the tidal creek down to the superb beach at 👁 **Traeth Mawr**. Head left along the sands to the far end of the bay, then turn left up through the dunes along a fence line to your right to reach the lane. Turn right along the lane.

The official route bears right along the quiet lane taking a direct line across the dunes. After a gentle rise, bear left with the lane, signed 'Malltraeth Newborough'. The lane continues, wooded for a section, near the **Bodorgan Estate**, and again a little further on.

Keep ahead at a fork ignoring a left to reach a crossroads on the edge of the village of **Hermon** with a fine view out over the estuary of **Afon Cefni** to the mountains of Snowdonia on the mainland. (The final section of road can be avoided by a permissinve path on the right running parallel to the lane.)

2 Turn right down '**Aberhoccwn Lane**', which leads down to the edge of the **Cefni estuary**. About 100 metres short of the road end, turn left onto a concrete access road. After about 150 metres bear right onto an enclosed footpath under low trees across a wet area by boardwalks. Keep left at a fork following an enclosed footpath and turn right at a junction to reach an **access road**. Cross the road and take the path opposite down towards the estuary. Just before the marshy shore, turn left through narrow **stone gateposts** and follow a path along the bottom of gardens. **Boardwalks** cross wet areas and as you approach the **village of Malltraeth** the path becomes enclosed between gardens to emerge in the village centre. Turn right and walk down to the **river**.

Malltraeth takes its name from the nearby estuary of Afon Cefni—traeth meaning 'beach' or 'shore'. Large as the estuary is today, originally it reached inland for over 12 miles to the outskirts of Llangefni. Like Traeth Mawr near Porthmadog, reclamation schemes at the beginning of the nineteenth century turned much of the estuary into the farmland we see today. This was accomplished by means of the seawall or 'cob', which spans the estuary between here and the Newborough Forest. This scheme enabled Thomas Telford to route his new coach road (what is now the A5) across what then would have been tidal marshes.

On the seaward side of the 'cob' the estuary is little altered and it was this vast stretch of tidal sands that provided the inspiration for much of the work of the late wildlife illustrator Charles Tunnicliffe. He was born in 1901 in eastern Cheshire and moved to Malltraeth with his wife in 1947. His house 'Shorelands', looked out over the estuary and provided the naturalist with enough material to last him a dozen lifetimes. He died at Malltraeth in 1979.

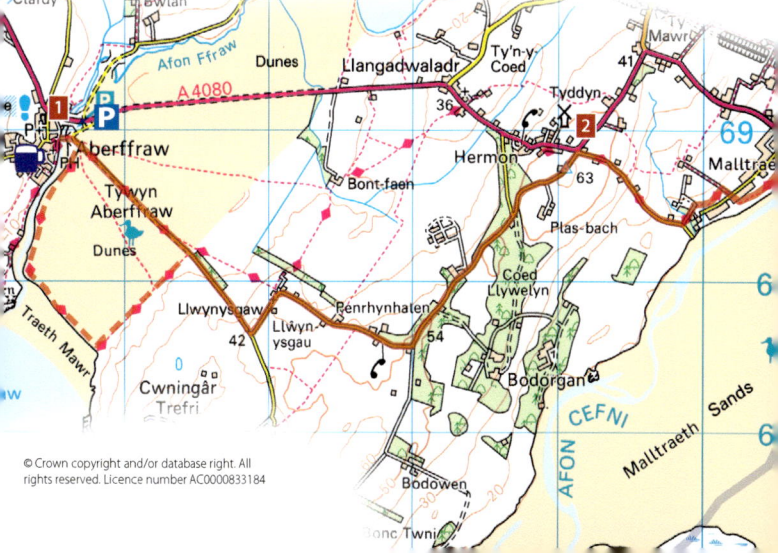

© Crown copyright and/or database right. All rights reserved. Licence number AC0000833184

Sea view: *Newborough Forest looks out across the bay to the mountains of Snowdonia*

The estuary is of national importance to the numerous species of wildfowl which stop to feed here on their long migratory flights between Arctic Norway and Africa.

3 From **Malltraeth** cross the bridge and bear right onto the seawall or 'cob' which is about 1.6 kilometres/1 mile long.

At the far end of the cob the path leads into one of the **car parks** for the 👁 **Newborough Forest**. Walk through the car park and take the path ahead parallel to the road.

4 At the main **forest road** in around 250 metres turn right. Follow the broad forest road for about 1.6 kilometres/1 mile.

Newborough Forest was planted in the 1950s to stabilise a vast area of moving sand dunes formed over the last 700 years by prevailing southwesterly winds. Today, it is a working forest and has been designated as a Site of Special Scientific Interest (SSSI).

The trees, mainly Corsican Pine, thrive in the sandy soil and are not harmed by the salt spray thrown up during winter storms. They have stabilised the dunes which have suffered frequent erosion problems over the centuries. As early as Elizabethan times, attempts to stabilise the dunes by planting marram grass were made after over-grazing damaged the thin soil cover. This led to vast areas of valuable agricultural land, that had been farmed since the Middle Ages, being buried by several metres of wind-blown sand.

The introduction of marram grass gave rise to a thriving cottage industry making ropes, baskets and mats which continued until the end of the last century. Today the lime-rich soil (from tiny shell fragments) of the older inland dunes, produces a colourful display of wild flowers in the spring and summer. This sensitive area is now protected and walkers are reminded to keep to the designated rights of way to avoid further erosion.

5 At the first track on the right (about 1 mile into the forest at **post number 17**) turn right as signed for the coast path. This track heads out towards the edge of the woods.

6 Close to the edge of the plantations, follow the signed coast path on the left. This undulates through the trees near the edge of the forest eventually making a short descent. Keep ahead on the sandy path to join a broader forest track at **post 14**. Take the left fork here and stay on this broad forest road for about 1.5 kilometres/1 mile.

A glimpse of Ynys Llanddwyn through the dunes

Spectacular beach: *The wide sweep of Traeth Penrhos and its extensive sand dunes*

Alternative route: *Along the beach*

Alternatively, by keeping ahead at point 6 you can walk this section on the salt marsh, dunes and the beach (**Traeth Penrhos**) to Ynys Llanddwyn. This is a little harder under foot than the forest option but the views are far more dramatic. The path out across the saltmarsh can be muddy, but the section through the dunes and along the beach as it curves around the vast expanse of Traeth Penrhos is straightforward. Keep an eye out for the remains of a shipwreck in the sand. Known locally as 'Y llong Groeg'—'the Greek Ship', it is the remains of the brig *'Athena'*, which foundered en-route to Liverpool in 1852. Fourteen crew were saved by the Llanddwyn lifeboat.

If you walked the beach option you will most likely do the short circuit of 👁 **Ynys Llanddwyn** too. Continue along the following beach (Traeth Llanddwyn) to the end of the plantations and locate a footpath on the left which runs along the edge of the trees with the dunes of **Newborough Warren** to the right.

7 Back on the **official route**, turn right at a T-junction. This forest road descends for around 400 metres, then curves left and begins to rise. Turn

Section 11: **Aberffraw to Newborough** 171

right in about 100 metres or so at **post number 5** onto a forest path. This emerges at a small **car park** by the beach.

> **Detour**: *To visit Ynys Llanddwyn*
> Turn right just as the forest road curves right (and before you reach the right turn at **post number 5**) onto a sandy path which leads down onto the beach. Bear right now towards the island in front of you. A path which begins beside the information board will take you to the southern

Pilots' cottages

These cottages once housed the Llanddwyn Pilots and their families. They ran the lighthouse and guided shipping into Caernarfon harbour. They also acted as lifeboatmen and the small cannon in front of the cottages was used to summon the lifeboat crew in times of distress. The Pilots' Cottages were renovated in 1977 by Anglesey Borough Council and two are regularly open to the public.

The old lighthouse, cross and pony on Ynys Llanddwyn

Lovers' island

Ynys Llanddwyn is an idyllic tidal island just off Newborough Warren

Remote and unspoilt, Ynys Llanddwyn is undoubtedly a special place. Cut off from the mainland by only the highest tides, the low-lying rocky headland pushes into the sea at the southern entrance to the Menai Strait. Its ancient lighthouses, ruined church, stone crosses and holy well, pilots' cottages and secluded bays all add to the romance.

But the island's main claim to fame is as the home of St Dwynwen, a 5th-century princess spurned in love, who later became the 'patron saint of lovers'. She is the Welsh equivalent of Saint Valentine and her Saint's Day on the 25th January is still celebrated across Wales with cards and flowers.

Today, the island is part of the extensive Newborough Warren National Nature Reserve, which includes Newborough Forest with its red squirrels and ravens, and the beaches, estuary and wildflower-rich dune system.

Flowers found on the island include thrift, bird's-foot trefoil, sea holly and yello horned poppies. Waders such as sandpipers, turnstones and little ringed plovers hunt the shore while terns and cormorants fish just offshore.

More information: To learn more about the island, visit the free museum housed in the Old Pilots' Cottages at the tip of Llanddwyn Island.

Section 11: **Aberffraw to Newborough** 173

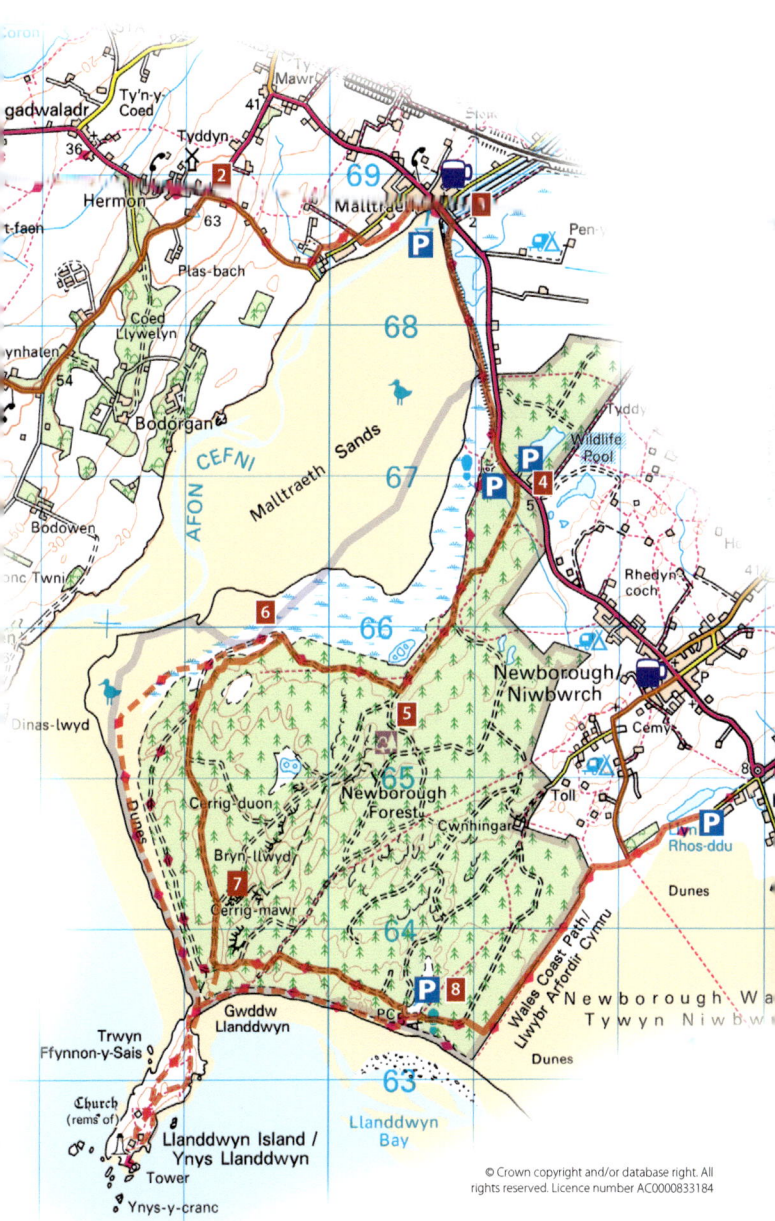

tip of the island where the lighthouse stands and the renovated Pilots' Cottages can be viewed.

The smaller white tower down to the left was originally a navigation beacon built in 1819. In 1972, this structure was found to be more suitable for the modern automatic beacon than the later lighthouse which is now disused.

Today, spectacular scenery and miles of secluded beach are the main attraction for the visitor. To the south, the serrated outlines of Snowdonia, followed by the blue silhouettes of Yr Eifl (The Rivals) and the smaller hills of Llŷn form an impressive backdrop to the wide sweep of Caernarfon Bay and the golden sands of Traeth Llanddwyn.

From the old lighthouse, a good footpath leads along the southern edge of the island passing the ruins of **Eglwys Dwynwen** on the right.

These are the ruins of a sixteenth century church dedicated to Saint Dwynwen, said to be built on the site of her original church established over 1,000 years earlier. The arched windows are edged with sandstone blocks and the outline of a small churchyard can be traced in the grass outside the building. The present ruinous state of the church is said have been due in

The old lighthouse, Ynys Llanddwyn

Section 11: **Aberffraw to Newborough** 175

Car park art: *Sculptures depicting bundles of marra grass once used by locals for basket making*

part to the removal of timbers for boat building and stone for the navigation beacon at the beginning of the nineteenth century.

Return to the information board where you came onto the island and turn right along the beach, then bear left up off the beach back through the small car park.

Back on the **official route**, turn left and follow the road out of the car park and follow the forest road curving right through the woods to the large **main car park for Newborough Forest and beach**.

8 Go ahead through the car park past the **information boards**. At the far side, turn left, then right on the signed coastal path out of the car park and into the dunes. Follow the path through a more open area where the trees have retreated as the dunes have eroded. Just after the path swings round to the left, turn right by a marker post onto a forest path.

Almost at the edge of the plantations, turn left and follow a path along the edge of the forest. As you leave the forest behind bear right along a narrow access track. This swings left in about 200 metres. To finish at **Newborough** follow this tack left to join a lane and continue to the village (approximately 1.6 kilometres/1 mile). Alternatively, keep ahead on the footpath to reach the small **parking area at Llyn Rhos-ddu**.

12 Section twelve

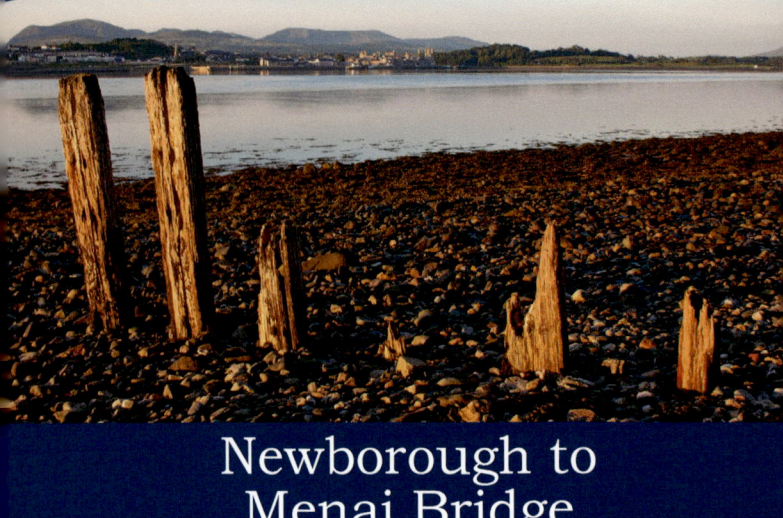

Newborough to Menai Bridge

Distance: *18.5km/11½ miles* | **Start:** *Llyn Rhos-ddu SH 426 640*
Finish: *Menai Bridge SH 537 715* | **Maps:** *Ordnance Survey263, Landranger 114*

Outline: A mixed section, initially through farmland then along the Menai Strait by the shoreline, field paths and quiet lanes

This section is almost completely flat. After stepping stones across one of the island's main rivers—Afon Braint—the path passes through a mixture of low-level farmland and foreshore. Reaching the Menai Strait the character of walk changes. Quiet lanes alternate with field paths and occasional detours onto the foreshore. There are good views to the mainland across the Menai Strait and the landscape is particularly attractive as it narrows and becomes more wooded. A long unavoidable inland detour is neccessary around the large house and grounds of Plas Newydd, but this does give you chance to visit the restored burial chamber of Bryn Celi Ddu. The final couple of miles are along the shore of the Strait passing beneath Anglesey's two famous bridges.

Services: *Not much on the route all the way to Menai Bridge, however Foel Farm and Anglesey Sea Zoo have cafés and provide ideal mid-walk breaks.*

👁 **Don't miss: Afon Briant stepping stones** – massive stepping stones | **Bryn Celi Ddu Burial Chamber** – An important reconstructed prehistoric monument | **Plas Newydd** – National Trust stately home overlooking the Menai Strait

▲ *The remains of old jetties at Tal y Foel*

Newborough

The village of Newborough came into existence in 1303, to accommodate the villagers evicted from Llanfaes, over in the east of the island, when Edward I began the building of his new garrison town and castle at Beaumaris. The move created a 'new borough' from which the village gets its name.

This site was chosen because it was previously poor unused land but its exposed location soon created problems for the villagers. Over-grazing and the removal of trees on the nearby dunes of Newborough Warren damaged the delicate soil cover and by the time of Elizabeth I, wind-blown sand had buried much of the village's valuable agricultural land.

In an attempt to stabilise the dunes, marram grass was introduced which, in the nineteenth century, gave rise to the flourishing basket and rope making industry. The area remained problematic however, and in the late 1940s Newborough Forest was planted. As a working forest it produced over 10,000 tonnes of timber per year, but the site is ecologically valuable. Since 2004 moves have been made to reduce forested areas and improve the area's biodiversity. Red squirrel numbers have increased and can often be seen at the Parc Mawr site.

The distant hills of Llŷn seen from the Menai Strait

Hop, skip and a jump: *Crossing Afon Braint by the historic stepping stones*

The route: **Llyn Rhos-ddu to Menai Bridge**

1 From the car park, walk to the mini roundabout on the main road. Go straight ahead here following the road (there is a pavement on the left-hand side). In about 300 metres, where the pavement ends, cross over and turn right into an access road. This road is very straight and runs for over 1km/½ mile giving access to a few farms and cottages. At the end of the lane beyond a gate a footpath continues down to the tidal river—**Afon Braint**.

2 The river can be crossed easily by 👁 **large stepping stones** (try to avoid crossing the stones at high tide as they do sometimes become submerged). On the far side turn left along a boardwalk then follow the path beside a wall parallel to the river.

Where the river curves away to your left, two kissing gates take you over an **embankment** ahead. Head directly across the next two fields and in the third field turn right immediately through a kissing gate to follow an enclosed path. At the end of the path go through a gate into an open field and walk ahead up the field edge. In the right-hand corner go through a kissing gate and along a hedged path on the right. This soon turns left up to reach a junction of farm tracks. Turn right and follow the track past outbuildings.

3 Go through a gate into the garden of a house, **Cae Llechau**, and turn left down the drive. As the drive swings off to the right, bear left to cross a stone stile into a field. Walk ahead up the left-hand edge of the field to a gate into a lane. Turn right along the lane.

4 In about 75 metres, turn left down the driveway to the house **Tan Tŵr**. Follow the left-hand driveway and go through a gate into fields. Walk down the left edge of the field and through a kissing gate almost in the bottom left-hand corner. Go ahead across a small field to join a farm track. Follow this to a lane and turn right along the lane.

5 In about 1 kilometre/¾ mile (shortly after **Tal Gwynedd** house and grounds) turn left along an access road on a right-hand bend. Walk along the access road and just before you reach a **house** turn right over a ladder stile. Walk down two fields, through a small gate and down steps onto the shore of the **Menai Strait**.

This is a lovely quiet spot on the rocky shore of the Menai Strait with views across to Caernarfon with the old castle backed by the mountains of Snowdonia.

The modern town of Caernarfon was founded by Edward I in the thirteenth century when he built one of Wales' most famous castles, along with a new fortified town. It controlled the southern entrance to the Menai Strait as Beaumaris would control its northern approach. It remained an important town during the Middle Ages and a number of ferries linked the town with Anglesey prior to the building of Telford's suspension bridge in 1826. One or two of these remained in use long after the bridge was built, including the Tal y Foel ferry which continued to operate until 1954.

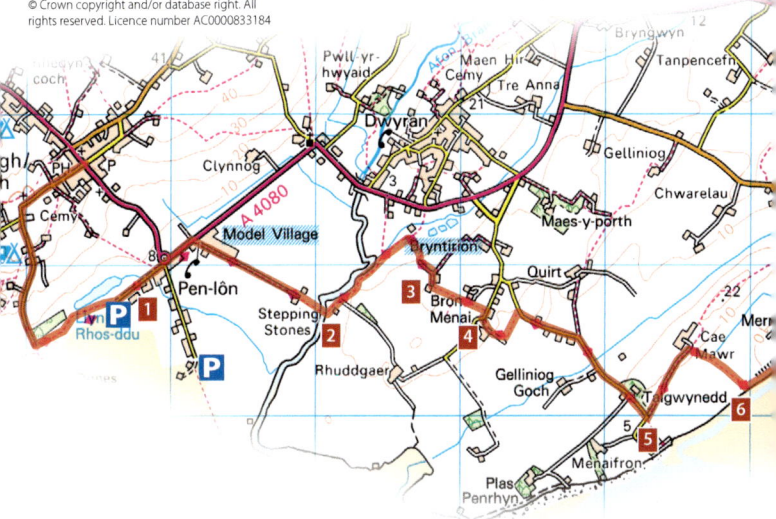

© Crown copyright and/or database right. All rights reserved. Licence number AC0000833184

Strait and narrow: *The broad western end of the Menai Strait*

6 Turn left along the pebbly shore and follow it to reach the lane at **Tal y Foel pier** (if the tide is high you can continue along an inland path past 'Cae Mawr' to 'Cerrig y Barcud' and then down the lane).

Walk ahead along the road parallel to the Menai Strait. Pass **Foel Farm Parc** and **Anglesey Sea Zoo** (both have a café) and continue until the road turns left away from the shore by cottages at '**Barras Bach**'.

7 Walk down onto the shingle beach here and after about 100 metres turn left where steps and a kissing gate take you into a field. Bear right along the field edge. Go through a kissing gate about 50 metres out from the field corner and head directly through the following large fields following a line of kissing gates until you enter an **area of scrub and trees**. The well-worn path keeps to the left edge of the woods until a kissing gate takes you into a large field. Walk directly through the field to enter a quiet lane.

8 Turn right down the lane to small roundabout beside the ruins of **Llanidan church** on the right.

The ruins of the church are visible through the gate but the church is not open to the public. It dates from the fourteenth century although the dedication—to Saint Nidan—is much older, probably from as early as the seventh century. The

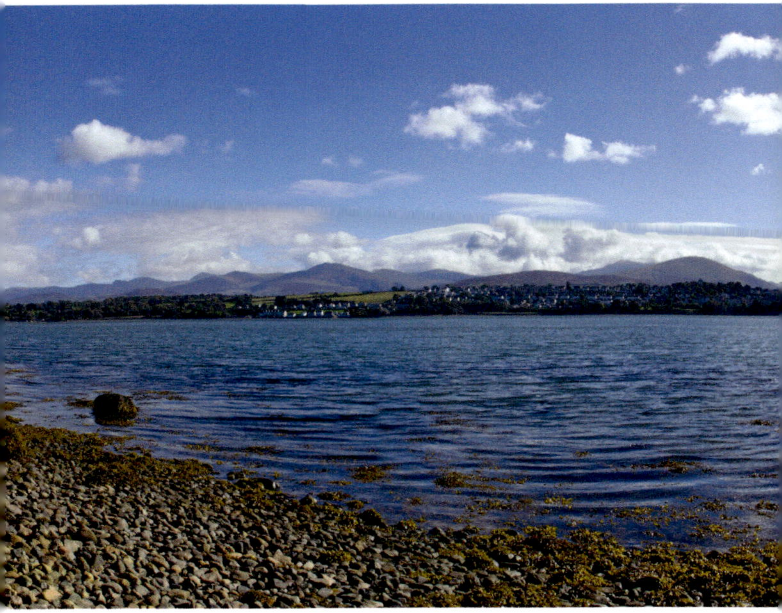

church was partly demolished in 1844, but prior to that served much of the area around Brynsciencyn.

There are **two official routes** from here:

For the **coastal option** which may have tidal restrictions, bear right at the roundabout and follow the track past the church down towards the Menai Strait. Just above the shore the track bears left down onto the shingle. Walk along the shore for about 1 kilomtre/¾ mile.

Llyfrgell Genedlaethol Cymru / National Library of Wales

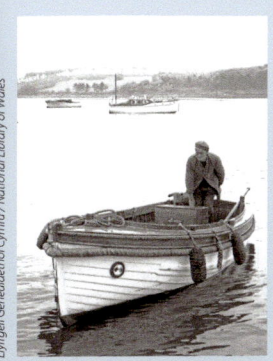

Menai ferries

For centuries, Moel-y-don was the site of one of the many ferries providing Anglesey with a link to the mainland. It was from the jetty here that Anglesey quarrymen were taken across to Y Felinheli where they caught a train to the Dinorwig slate quarries. The last ferryman at Moel-y-don, Edward Owen, carried passengers across the Strait in this traditional wooden boat until the late 1950s.

Telford's famous Menai suspension bridge

Menai Strait

The narrow Menai Strait separates Anglesey from mainland North Wales

Sometimes referred to locally as the *Afon Menai* or 'River Menai', the Menai Strait is a narrow stretch of shallow tidal water roughly 15 miles/ 24 kilometres long that separates the Isle of Anglesey from mainland North Wales. It extends from Trwyn Penmon, in the north-east, to Abermenai Point—opposite Caernarfon Castle—in the south-west, and varies in width from 2 miles/ 3 kilometres at either end to just 200 yards/180 metres at the Swellies, the dramatic central stretch between the Britannia Bridge and Menai Bridge.

The Strait is actually a submerged geological fault, gouged out by a succession of glacial ice sheets over many thousands of years and then flooded as global sea levels rose at the end of the last Ice Age.

Aerial view of Church Island, Menai Strait

Tidal flows in the Strait are complex and dramatic. Incoming tides first enter the Strait at the south-west end to flow northwards. But before the water can reach the far end, it is met head on by a second tidal wave (which has travelled faster in the deep water around the top of Anglesey) pushing in from the north-eastern end at Trwyn Penmon. Depending on wind and tidal conditions, the two opposing flows meet somewhere in the middle, causing white water, whirlpools and fierce currents of up to 8 knots.

Menai's Nelson statue was erected in 1873 by an artist experimenting with concrete

Yet, despite the danger, the Menai Strait has always been a busy short cut for ships sailing between Cardigan Bay and the Irish Sea. However, while it was safe to traverse the Strait at slack water, catch the tide wrong and you were in trouble. One of the most dangerous sections is around the Swellies (or 'Swillies', from the Welsh *Pwll Ceris*) where rocks just beneath the surface cause overfalls and whirlpools. This was where the training ship *HMS Conway* was lost in 1953.

Crossing the Strait was dangerous too. So it was a relief for passengers when the Thomas Telford's famous suspension bridge was built in 1827, followed by Robert Stephenson's Britannia tubular railway bridge in 1849. Rebuilt with a second deck carrying the A55 after a disastrous fire in 1970, the Pont Britannia still carries thousands of trains and road going vehicles across the Menai Strait each year. Plans are discussed for a third Menai crossing.

> *"The 15 miles of river-like channel, overhung by quiet inland woods, yet fringed along their shores with seaweed, is a paradox of Nature that cannot but rouse the scientific imagination."*
>
> *Edward Greenly,* geologist, 1910

More information: For more details of the Menai Strait, its geology, history, wildlife and culture, see: https://en.wikipedia.org/wiki/Menai_Strait

Leave the shore through a kissing gate (opposite a ruined stone quay) to join an old grassy track. This rises up through a field to emerge on the corner of a lane just south of the large house, **Plas Porthamel**.

9 Turn right along the lane and follow it with views across the Menai Strait to the right for about 1 kilometre/¾ mile. At a T-junction turn left and walk up to the main road. (A right turn at the T-junction will take you down to the **Moel-y-don** car park on the edge of the Menai Strait.)

Tidal alternative: For the inland alternative, turn left at the roundabout beside Llanidan church up the narrow lane overhung with trees and at the top of the rise, take the first lane on the right indicated by the 'coastal path' sign.

This quiet lane is high enough above the Menai Strait to allow a good view down to the water—which has the appearance of a large inland river rather than the sea—and across to the mountains on the mainland.

Continue along the lane and when this bears right to the farm at '**Meini Gwynion**', continue straight ahead on a grassy track. At a fork keep right and bear right near farm buildings at '**Plas Porthamel**'. Follow the lane and turn left at a bend ignoring a track straight ahead (the shore option comes out here). Turn left at the next junction and walk up to the main road. Continue from Point 10.

10 A the crossroads take the lane opposite and follow it for about 1 kilometre/¾ mile.

The reconstructed Neolithic burial chamber at Bryn Celli Ddu

Section 12: **Newborough to Menai Bridge** 185

11 Immediately before the 'Llandaniel' sign, take the footpath on the right signed to 👁 **Bryn Celli Ddu Neolithic Burial Chamber**. This path is enclosed and runs between fields to a footbridge on the left. (To visit the burial chamber take the path left over the bridge, but you will to return to this point to continue.)

12 To continue go ahead over a small **footbridge** and through a gate into a large field. Keep ahead beside the stream for about 300m to a stile and footbridge on the left. Don't cross this, instead bear half-right across the field to pass through a kissing gate in the far fence between two woods. In the following field bear half-right again to go through a kissing gate in the far corner. *There is a grand view ahead from here to the mountains of Snowdonia including Snowdon itself.* Turn left along the field edge now to eventually reach the access drive to a **farm** on the

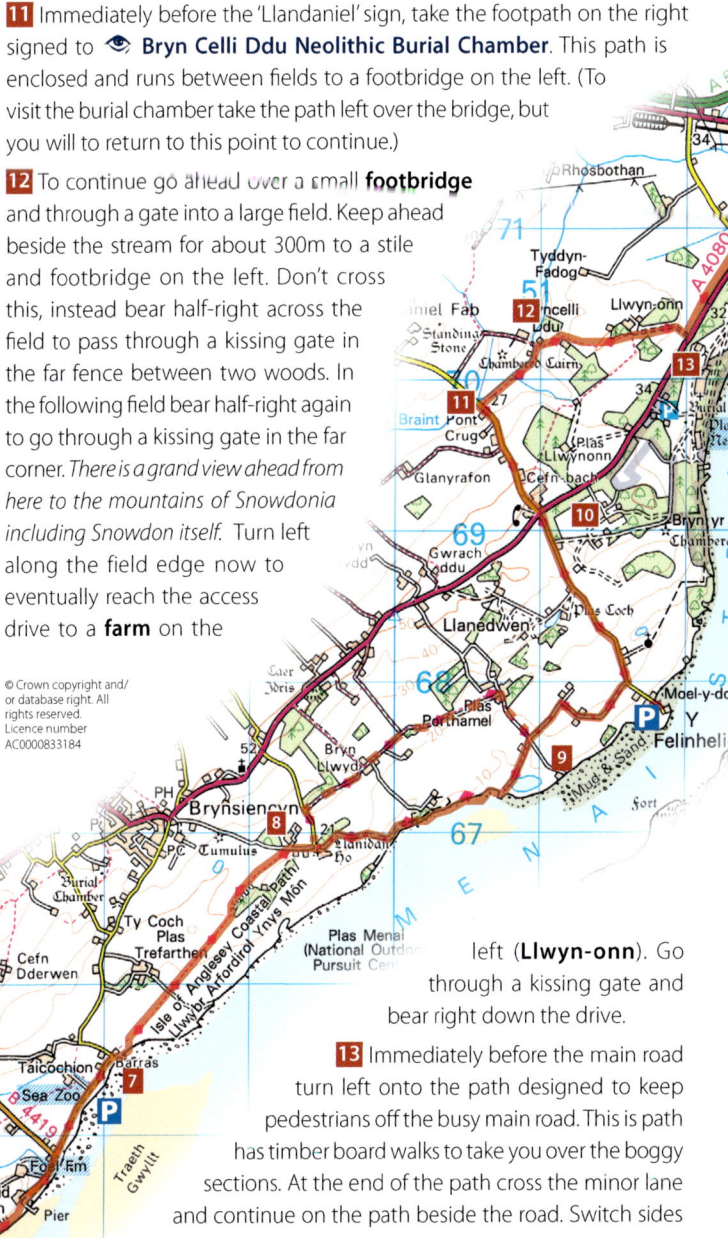

© Crown copyright and/or database right. All rights reserved. Licence number AC0000833184

left (**Llwyn-onn**). Go through a kissing gate and bear right down the drive.

13 Immediately before the main road turn left onto the path designed to keep pedestrians off the busy main road. This is path has timber board walks to take you over the boggy sections. At the end of the path cross the minor lane and continue on the path beside the road. Switch sides

Intimate knowledge: *Nelson's statue stands eyeing the stretch of water he knew well*

a little further on, shortly passing one of the entrances to 👁 **Plas Newydd**, stately home, now owned by the National Trust. Cross the footbridge over the stream and rise to reach a lane.

Turn right down the lane. At a sharp right-hand bend by the water treatment works bear left through an **arched gate** in the wall and follow a path down through woodland to emerge on the shore of the **Menai Strait** beside the houses at **Pwll-fangol**.

14 At the end of the path go down steps onto a **raised stone walkway** above the shore. Cross a **jetty** and continue along the walkway. Cross the **sailing club slipway** and where the walkway ends bear left following the path beside a fenced boat compound. At the end of the fence turn right down stone steps onto the shore. **Be aware that this is a permissive route and is only open during daylight hours, or between 7am and 9pm (whichever comes first).** Turn left along the shore past **Nelson's statue**.

The statue of Admiral Lord Nelson was erected as a marker for shipping in the 1850s by Lord Clarence Paget, son of the Marquis. Nelson knew this stretch of water well and considered it to be one of the most difficult to navigate. He is reputed to have remarked that 'whoever could navigate a sailing ship through the Menai Strait could sail any sea in the world'.

With just 10 metres of water, a rocky uneven floor and so little room to manoeuvre it seems incredible that anyone should try and bring a large sailing ship this way but ships did pass through the Strait quite regularly and when Thomas Telford built his new suspension bridge in 1826 its tremendous height—over 100 feet—was set to enable sailing ships to pass.

Just after the statue cross **stepping stones** over the stream, then bear left up a path through the cemetery of **Saint Mary's church** to come out at the car park.

Follow the road up past the **old rectory** and under the railway bridge. Turn right immediately after the railway bridge onto a wide track beside the car park for '**Carreg Brân Hotel**'. Pass beneath the **Britannia Bridge** and follow the track down to the shore. At the shore turn left through a gap in the wall and walk along a well-defined path through an area of woodland owned by the National Trust at **Coedmôr**. This is a surprisingly lovely section along the wooded shore with views across to the mainland.

Ignore a public footpath going off to the left, continuing ahead to reach a fenced path at the bottom of a field. Follow this path ahead through a gate (ignore the path up to a viewpoint on the left) and continue to go through a kissing gate. The path heads along the bottom of the following field and then up a fenced path to reach the road. Turn right along the road towards **Menai Bridge**.

Heavy traffic: *Stevenson's Britannia Bridge carries both rail and road traffic onto the island*

15 Just before the roundabout, turn right down an access road to the **Rugby Club**. Bear right through a kissing gate and along a fenced path around the rugby pitch. You will come out by the access to **Saint Tysilio's church** on a little island to the right.

Ignore this (unless you want to visit the church) and carry straight on along the **Belgian Promenade**. At the lane turn left up to the main road to complete the coast path.

Congratulations!

Wales Coast Path: Official Guides

The **Official Guides** to the **Wales Coast Path** are endorsed by Natural Resources Wales, the Welsh government body which developed and manage the path. The guides break the Wales Coast Path into seven main sections, giving long-distance and local walkers everything they need to enjoy all 870 miles of this world-class route. **Buy online at: www.northerneyebooks.co.uk**

North Wales Coast
Chester to Bangor
ISBN: 978-1-914589-00-3

Llŷn Peninsula
Bangor to Porthmadog
ISBN: 978-1-914589-02-7

Snowdonia Coast & Ceredigion Coast
Porthmadog to Cardigan
ISBN: 978-1-914589-03-4

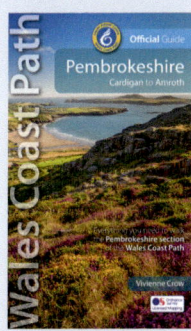

Pembrokeshire
Cardigan to Amroth
ISBN: 978-1-908632-98-2

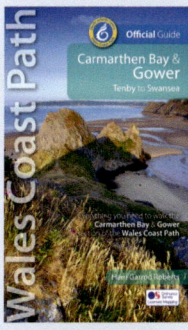

Carmarthen Bay & Gower *Tenby to Swansea*
ISBN: 978-1-908632-99-9

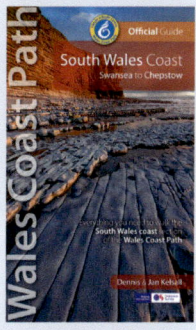

South Wales Coast
Swansea to Chepstow
ISBN: 978-1-914589-04-1

Access to large scale Ordnance Survey mapping

A major new feature of the website offers access to **large scale Ordnance Survey mapping** showing the route for each official Day Section. This can be used on a smart phone, along with the locator feature, to find and follow the users' position at any point on the path.

Major **new features** have been added to the website including:

Online **Ordnance Survey large scale mapping** with position locator

A major new **accommodation booking** feature at the end of each Day Section

Accommodation booking

A new accommodation booking feature has been added to the website enabling quick, easy booking for a range of accommodation at the beginning and end of each official Day Section on any of the seven sections of the Wales Coast Path.

In addition, you will be able to book a range of local day trips and transport options—including national and international flights, and vehicle hire.

Wales Coast Path: Large scale mapping atlas

Detailed 1:25,000 scale **Ordnance Survey** mapping for each of the seven sections of the Wales Coast Path for use with the Official Guides in a handy, easy-to-use, pocket size book format. The official route is overprinted in a yellow wash line and the end of each day secion is clearly marked, along with additional information such as WC facilitites, pubs and cafés close to the route.

Buy online at: www.northerneyebooks.co.uk

Currently available

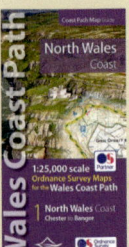

1: North Wales Coast: *Chester to Bangor*
1:25,000 OS mapping for the Wales Coast Path

80 miles/125 kilometres of superb coastal walking. Dee estuary, traditional seaside towns, Great Orme and Conwy Mountain.

ISBN 978-1-908632-58-6

40pp | 210 x 110mm | Softback, flapped cover

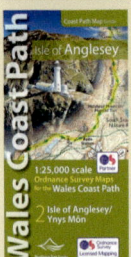

2: Isle of Anglesey: *Bangor to Menai Bridge*
1:25,000 OS mapping for the Wales Coast Path

130 miles/210 kilometres of superb coastal walking. Grand coastal scenery from tidal strait to bhays, estuaries, dunes and cliffs. AONB.

ISBN 978-1-908632-59-3

48pp | 210 x 110mm | Softback, flapped cover

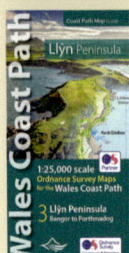

3: Llyn Peninsula: *Bangor to Porthmadog*
1:25,000 OS mapping for the Wales Coast Path

110 miles/180 kilometres of superb coastal walking. Unspoilt peninsula with bays, coves and cliffs, tipped by Bardsey Island. AONB.

ISBN 978-1-908632-60-9

48pp | 210 x 110mm | Softback, flapped cover

Wales Coast Path: Top 10 Walks

Award-winning pocket-size walking guides to the most popular, easy circular walks along key sections of the Wales Coast Path. The full series will cover the whole path in ten attractive guides.

Buy online at: www.northerneyebooks.co.uk

Currently available

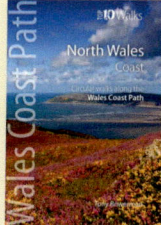

**Top 10 Walks:
North Wales Coast**
ISBN: 978-1-908632-15-9

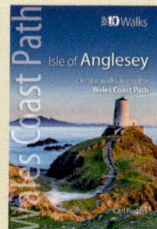

**Top 10 Walks:
Isle of Anglesey**
ISBN: 978-1 902512-31-0

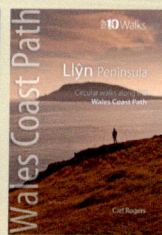

**Top 10 Walks:
Llyn Peninsula**
ISBN: 978-1-902512-34-1

**Top 10 Walks:
Snowdonia Coast**
ISBN: 978-1 908632-85-2

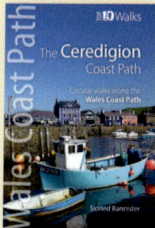

**Top 10 Walks:
The Ceredigion Coast**
ISBN: 978-1-908632-28-9

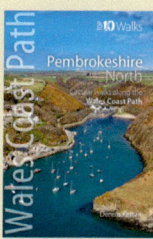

**Top 10 Walks:
Pembrokeshire North**
ISBN: 978-1-908632-29-6

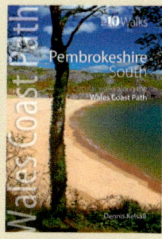

**Top 10 Walks:
Pembrokeshire South**
ISBN: 978-1 908632-30-2

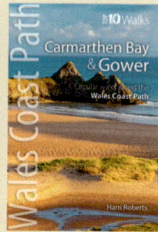

**Top 10 Walks:
Carmarthenshire & Gower**
ISBN: 978-1-908632-16-6

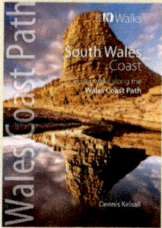

**Top 10 Walks:
South Wales Coast**
ISBN: 978-1-908632-31-9

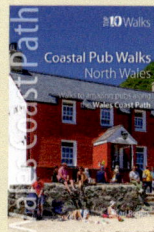

**Top 10 Walks:
Coastal Pub Walks
North Wales**
ISBN: 978-1 908632-82-1

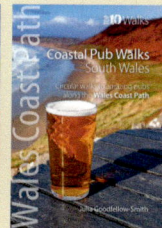

**Top 10 Walks: Coastal
Pub Walks
South Wales**
ISBN: 978-1-914589-15-7

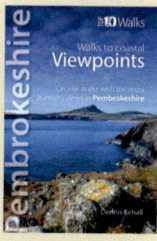

**Top 10 Walks: Walks to
Coatal Viewpoints
Pembrokeshire**
ISBN: 978-1-908632-93-7

Useful Information

Wales Coast Path

Comprehensive information about all sections of the Wales Coast Path can be found on the official website at: **www.walescoastpath.gov.uk** and **www.walescoastpath.co.uk**.

'Visit Wales'

The Visit Wales website covers everything from accommodation to attractions. For information on the area covered by this book, see: **www.visitwales.com/explore/north-wales/anglesey**

Isle of Anglesey

For local information about Anglesey, from what to see and do to eating out and where to stay, see **www.visitanglesey.co.uk/en**.

Tourist Information Centres

There are no longer any full time TICs on Anglesey, just a few part time 'local information points'.

Where to stay

There's plenty of accommodation close to the Wales Coast Path on Anglesey, from campsites and B&Bs to holiday cottages and hotels. Most can be booked online. **To book accommodation at the end of each Day Section, visit the 'Plan Your Walk' section at: www.walescoastpath.co.uk**

Walking holidays

The following companies offer complete walking packages for the Wales Coast Path on Anglesey, including accommodation, local information, maps, baggage transfer and transport.

Anglesey Walking Holidays 01248 713 611|
www. angleseywalkingholidays.com | info@angleseywalkingholidays.com
Celtic Trails 01291 689774 | www.celtic-trails.com | info@celtic-trails.com
Contours Walking Holidays 01629 821 900 | www.contours.co.uk | info@contours.co.uk

Train and buses

For public transport information across Wales, see **Traveline Cymru**. 0871 200 22 33 |**www.traveline.cymru**

Trains for Holyhead on Anglesey depart from Chester, Crewe, Birmingham and Cardiff.

For train times and tickets, see **Arriva Trains Wales** www.arrivatrainswales.co.uk or National Rail Enquiries www.nationalrail.co.uk. Local bus services on the island can be found at: www.anglesey.gov.uk/transport-and-roads/public-transport/bus-or-coach/local-bus-timetables/. For downloadable timetables, use the journey planner on www.traveline.cymru.

Taxis

LlanfairPG	PG Cars	01248 716503
Rhosneigr	RhosneigrTaxi Co	07723 373176
Amlwch	Annie's Cabs	07784 075363
Beaumaris	Beaumaris Cars	07989 431935
Holyhead	Marks Taxis	01407 721222

Cycle hire

Cycle Wales Llangefni Golf Course, Clai Rd, Llangefni LL77 7TJ | 01248 724787 | www.cyclewales.net

Evolution Bikes Cyttir Lane, Bangor LL57 4DA | 01248 355770 | www.evolution-bikes.co.uk

Boat Trips

RibRide Fast RIB ride adventures. Menai Strait, Llanddwyn Island, Holyhead and the Skerries. | 0333 1234 303 | **www.ribride.co.uk** | info@ribride.co.uk

Seawake Anglesey Boat Trips Explore coastal Anglesey and the Menai Strait on a powerboat trip. Fast and slow boats including RIBs | 01248 716335 | **www.angleseyboattrips.com** | info@seawake.co.uk

Seacoast Safaris Puffin Island boat trips, RIB rides and round Anglesey tours. | 07854 028 393/ 07494 441 112 | **www.seacoastsafaris.co.uk** | enquiries@seacoastsafaris.co.uk

Emergencies

In an emergency, call 999 or 112 and ask for the service you require: Ambulance, Police, Fire or Coastguard.

Tides

Short stretches of the Wales Coast Path and some alternative routes are only accessible on a low or outgoing tide. Check tide times before you go. Tide table booklets are widely available from TICs and local shops for around £1. For today's local tide information for places around Anglesey, visit **www.tidetimes.org.uk** and choose your nearest location.

Weather forecasts

For reliable, up-to-date weather forecasts, see **www.bbc.co.uk/weather** or **www.metoffice.gov.uk/weather/uk**.

Annual events

Vintage Rally

Beaumaris Lifeboat Day - June

Great Strait Raft Run - Y Felinheli to Menai Bridge Pier raft race - June

Gottwood Festival Critically acclaimed, independent, boutique and intimate underground electronic music festival - June

Anglesey Farmers Market Quality food producers come together on the third Saturday of each month - June, July, August

Beaumaris Food Festival Discover the best of Welsh produce to international street food. - September

Publishing information

© Crown copyright 2024.
All rights reserved.

Ordnance Survey, OS, and the OS logos are registered trademarks, and OS Short Walks Made Easy is a trademark of Ordnance Survey Ltd.

© Crown copyright and database rights (2024) Ordnance Survey.

ISBN 978 0 319092 80 4
1st edition published by Ordnance Survey 2024.

ordnancesurvey.co.uk

While every care has been taken to ensure the accuracy of the route directions, the publishers cannot accept responsibility for errors or omissions, or for changes in details given. The countryside is not static: hedges and fences can be removed, stiles can be replaced by gates, field boundaries can alter, footpaths can be rerouted and changes in ownership can result in the closure or diversion of some concessionary paths. Also, paths that are easy and pleasant for walking in fine conditions may become slippery, muddy and difficult in wet weather.

If you find an inaccuracy in either the text or maps, please contact Ordnance Survey at os.uk/contact.

All rights reserved. No part of this publication may be reproduced, transmitted in any form or by any means, or stored in a retrieval system without either the prior written permission of the publisher, or in the case of reprographic reproduction a licence issued in accordance with the terms and licences issued by the CLA Ltd.

A catalogue record for this book is available from the British Library.

Milestone Publishing credits

Author: Dixe Wills

Series editor: Kevin Freeborn

Maps: Cosmographics

Design and Production: Patrick Dawson, Milestone Publishing

Printed in India by Replika Press Pvt. Ltd

Photography credits

Front cover: Malcolm Grey, Photography | Wilderness is a State of Mind.
Back cover: cornfield/Shutterstock.com.

All photographs supplied by the author ©Dixe Wills except page 6 Tom Wake (Ordnance Survey); pages 2, 3, 14, 20, 22, 30, 34 Kevin Freeborn; pages 39, 41 Suzy Dixon.

The following images were supplied by Shutterstock.com: Page 1 SadlerC1; 4, 54 CDK Photos; 4, 42 DBUK; 5, 68 claire Bullion; 7, 9 StevenDocwra; 13 Artush; 18 Ryan Noeker; 19 Dennis Jacobsen; 19 Jenny Cottingham; 24 Lukasz Michalczyk; 24 Simonas Minkevicius; 25 Edvard Mizsei; 25 Hector Ruiz Villar; 25 rock ptarmigan; 26 Richard Bowden; 33 sakharumoowan; 33 Stephan Morris; 33 Vinicius R. Souza; 33 WildlifeWorld; 40 R J Endall Photographer; 41 Erni; 41 guraydere; 41 Voodison328; 43 Peter R Foster IDMA; 44 Eagle_Watch; 46 Dsmile88; 46 LesiChkalll27; 47 Jiri Hrebicek; 47 Luka Hercigonja; 47 Rudmer Zwerver; 53 Agorca; 53 Fotokostic; 59 DJTaylor; 59 riet bloemen; 60 yackers1; 66, 67 Szczepan Klejbuk; 67 Jamie Hall; 69 James Norfolkboy; 70 MyriadLifePhoto; 73 Edgar Smislov; 73 rorue; 78 Cordeant Photography; 78 Martin Fowler; 79 SGR Wildlife Photography.

The following images were sourced via Wikimedia Commons: page 16 John Sutton / King's Lynn: across Tuesday Market Place; page 16 Paul Shreeve / True's Yard Museum, King's Lynn / CC BY-SA 2.0 page 23 Adrian S Pye / Hunstanton Hall; page 23 DJC Skellingthorpe at English Wikipedia, CC BY-SA 3.0; page 36 Julian Dowse / 'Hjordis' Lighted Beacon, Blakeney NNR / CC BY-SA 2.0.

The open expanses of Breydon Water, and its associated wet grassland, inter-tidal mudflats and salt marsh, can get exceptionally busy in winter, when thousands of golden plover, black-tailed godwit and wigeon arrive. Large numbers of lapwings and Bewick swans make their way to overwinter too, joining resident redshanks and avocets. The avocet was first used as the RSPB emblem in 1955.

All year round you may spot a little egret or two – a small white heron from the Mediterranean that was once a rarity in Britain but whose range has expanded greatly since the 1980s.

The boardwalk that runs below the castle walls affords an excellent view into and over Breydon Water's huge reed bed, a quite mesmerising sight. Birds you might hear or see calling from the reed tops are sedge warbler, reed bunting and reed warbler.

On the later stages of the walk, look out for wild roses growing in the hedgerows, producing wonderful red hips in the autumn.

Redshank

7 ▶ For a shortcut, and the 🚶 route, turn **right** here, reading on from **9**, point two.
▶ Otherwise, turn **left**, staying on the Angles Way. Go through a gate and head along a path beside Breydon Water to a pair of wooden gates in just over ⅓ mile.

8 ▶ Pass through both gates and walk 100 yards to where the path turns sharp right.
▶ Pause to admire the extensive views up and down Breydon Water before retracing your steps to the Angles Way signpost.

9 ▶ This time, turn **left** at the signpost.
▶ Pass through a kissing-gate onto a road, bearing **right** to pass the church.
▶ Stay on Church Road to return to the pub, or turn **right** along Butts Lane for the car park.

NATURE NOTES

Top left: reed beds
Left: avocet
Top: Bewick swan
Bottom: rose hips

5 ▸ At the crossways, go **right**, towards the castle, with a hedge on your left.
▸ Continue **ahead** between a hedge and the castle wall to reach a path junction just beyond the end of the wall.

6 ▸ Go **right** at the junction onto a long boardwalk with a large expanse of reeds to your left.
▸ Continue for over ⅓ mile to a path junction and an Angles Way sign.

🏛 Burgh Castle

Known today as one of the 'Saxon Shore forts', Burgh Castle (Gariannonum) is one of the nation's best-preserved remnants from the Roman occupation. The fort was built in the third century as part of a chain of coastal defences. These worked well until CE 367, when the Saxons, Picts and Scots coordinated their attacks and the forts began to fall one by one (english-heritage.org.uk and norfarchtrust.org.uk).

☆ Roman Cavalry

Burgh was garrisoned by a form of Roman cavalry known as Equites Stablesiani. There would have been room within the fort's high walls to house up to 500 soldiers and their horses – quite a considerable force if the garrison was at full strength. Working together with the fort at Caister-on-Sea, the cavalry guarded the Great Estuary, a natural point of entry for invaders and raiders.

5 Crossways — **6** Burgh Castle / Castle wall / Boardwalk — 1 mile — **7** Angles Way signpost — **9** Turn right and read on from

2 Start – arriving by car
- Turn **right**, in the direction of the sign, and walk past the car park.
- Continue **straight ahead** along a footpath to reach a square shelter in 350 yards, just before the church.

3 At the shelter, turn **left** between hedges for 75 yards to reach a T-junction between two kissing-gates (neither of which you go through).

4 Turn **left** along a path, passing an English Heritage information sign.
- Walk to a crossroads of paths in just over ¼ mile.

Walk 10 Burgh Castle